You Eat with Your Eyes

The Simplicity & Elegance of Presenting Food by Chef Edward G. Leonard, CMC, WGMC, AAC

First published in the United States of America in 2008, reprinted in 2012 by:
LTD Publishing LLC

Author: Chef Edward G. Leonard, CMC, WGMC, AAC
Production Chef: Jonathan Moosmiller, CEC
Pastry Assistant: Mariana Delgado Gambini
Art Direction, Design, Layout: Graham Walters
Photography: John Ormond
Editor: Elin Jeffords
Recipe Editor: Alice Thompson

ISBN-13: 978-0-9815729-0-1
ISBN-10: 0-9815729-0-1

Printed & Bound in Korea

LE CORDON BLEU®

You Eat with Your Eyes

The Simplicity & Elegance of Presenting Food by Chef Edward G. Leonard, CMC, WGMC, AAC

IV ## *Acknowledgements*

Special thanks to Chef Jonathan Moosmiller, CEC, for his passion and belief in all of our culinary adventures. He is a true executive sous chef.

Thank you to my brigade of chefs and cooks who make all I do possible, especially, Mike, Sarah, Hanna, Mariana, Nick, CJ, Big Joe, Jamie, Marco, Seymour, and Veronica.

This book is dedicated to my three children—Cosette, Edward, and Giancarlo—who inspire me daily. May cooking be in their hearts, and may they enjoy real food in a world gone mad with chemicals and lack of respect for what we put in our bodies every day.

Lastly my mom, a great home cook that taught me true comfort food; that any young chef could have learned from.

Table of Contents

Foreword

I received my first cooking lesson as far away from a professional setting as one can imagine. It was in the back of my family's two-room house in Southern China, a makeshift kitchen where my mother set up her wok and chopping block. I was her favorite audience and she was my favorite cook. And every late afternoon I would curl up under the kitchen table, breathlessly watching her prepare our evening meal. In retrospect, mom was the star of the first *Yan Can Cook* show!

Then one day—I must have been five or six at the time—my mom beckoned me as she was wielding the cleaver on some green vegetables. "If you want to watch, you should learn," she said. And I did. The lesson that day was a simple one. Good food, according to my mom, must contain three essential elements: it must look good, it must smell good, and of course, it must taste good.

Over the years, that simple lesson has served me well. Look, smell and taste—three simple, easy to remember words. They were re-enforced time and time again, by renowned cooking instructors and master chefs, from professional classrooms to the kitchens of some of the world's best restaurants. And now, thanks to my good friend Master Chef Edward Leonard, they are gracing the pages of this beautiful book.

You Eat with Your Eyes, the title says it all. When Chef (we who admire Edward can only refer to him by the name 'Chef') first outlined his ideas of this book to me, I knew that he had a winner. And when I finally saw the title, I was sure. I hope I am not aging him, Chef and I have known each other personally and professionally for years if not decades. I've had the privilege of working side-by-side with Chef on different occasions, and have served with him on professional panels in China and other venues.

As a certified master chef and award-winning cookbook author, Chef Leonard has always impressed me with his encyclopedic knowledge of good cooking in its many manifestations. During his tenure as the president of the American Culinary Federation and his triumphant tour with the Team USA at the International Culinary Olympics, Chef Leonard has repeatedly demonstrated his tremendous leadership and far-reaching vision in all aspects of the epicurean art.

Personally, I was particularly (and pleasantly) surprised by the interest and depth of his knowledge in Chinese cuisine, right down to the presentations. Let me say that such talent was well appreciated during the International Chinese Chefs Convention and I am glad to see that Chef is sharing his talents with his readers and fellow professionals.

From his simple, yet imaginative, ways of highlighting a salad to his plating techniques to showcase a festive dinner party, Chef Leonard is true to his reputation of a distinguished culinarian. Within these pages he shows off his legendary techniques in an easy-to-follow, step-by-step manner. I know I will treasure this book in my kitchen for years to come, and I am sure that anyone who feels passionate about good cooking and good food will do the same.

Good food must look good. We all eat with our eyes before we open our mouths. My mom would agree. She would probably wish she had thought of that title first.

Chef Martin Yan

Author and Host of *Yan Can Cook*

Introduction

Welcome to a unique and useful book that illustrates the art and craft of effectively presenting food. That people eat first with their eyes is a truism. Beautiful presentations and exquisite garnishes can make food into art.

Food, like fashion, is subject to changes, fads, and trends. In past years, we have experienced continental cuisine, nouvelle cuisine, comfort food, regional American food, fusion food, East-meets-West—the list goes on. The plating and presentation of the food is subject to the same whims.

The classic way of plating is to use the clock as a guide—starch at two o'clock, vegetables at four or five o'clock, the main protein at between eight and ten o'clock. Then came the placing of the garnish—tomato roses, carved olives and other vegetables, the ubiquitous bunch of parsley, even citrus slices on occasion.

In many years as a chef, my own style of presenting and plating food has definitely evolved. I have worked with, competed against, and eaten in the restaurants of many other fine chefs all over the world. These experiences have profoundly influenced my style and continue to re-ignite my passion to perfect my cuisine.

Still, despite all these influences, a few things have remained constant. First and foremost, the presentation on the plate, no matter how grand, should never take precedence over proper cooking techniques and essential flavors. Chefs have been called artists, perhaps because of temperament, but in many ways our craft is indeed an art. I have always believed that great moments in that art can only occur when discipline merges with emotional and culinary intelligence.

Creating true art on the plate with food does take passion. Creativity is the discipline to do what makes sense combined with the intelligence to focus first on flavor.

In culinary competitions there is a cold buffet program as well as a category called "hot presented cold." There are many hot food cook-offs, too, and chefs compete everywhere in the world in hot kitchens.

The cold culinary salon is where the emphasis on presentation began. The challenge with the "hot presented cold" category is that judges evaluate the display solely on the presentation since they do not eat or taste the food. Success lies with the ability to demonstrate, through food presentation alone, proper cooking techniques as well as flavors that speak out and say, "Eat and enjoy this dish."

Some chefs scoff at competitions, years of competing creates a discipline, a solid philosophy of food. I look at my 20-plus years of competing as continuing education that pushes me to become better at my craft while at the same time attaining the discipline that ensures success in my everyday job of cooking for my customers. Some in the industry see me as a very accomplished artist of food design; I look at myself as a cook who enjoys his work to the fullest. I strive daily to raise the bar by serving great-tasting cuisine that is first enjoyed by the eye. I create plate designs that yell "Flavor!" and "You are in for a treat."

Cooking and entertaining at home is a national pastime. The Food Network, cooking reality shows, and the availability of professional kitchen design and professional equipment for the home have a created a generation of "foodies" and new opportunities for those who simply love food.

The quality of both take-out and "speed scratch" products have made it easier than ever to enjoy meals in the comfort of our own homes. The desire to serve food like a chef is more prevalent than ever.

The canvas for all your presentations is the plate itself. For many years the standard round china plate was the optimum canvas for chefs. These days, the selection, the colors, the shapes and types of plates, make for an array of improved canvases that showcase food in a whole new way. All too often, however, both home cooks and professional chefs design the food to suit the china rather than focusing on the food first and using the china to complement it.

There can be as much visual interest in a potpie or a roast turkey dinner as there is in scallops layered with truffles. This exciting book will take you through the art of plating. The journey will begin by showing you some dishes from my menus and battery of recipes. We will start with the amuse-bouche, go on to salads, lunch plates, first plates, main plates, pastry, and even family-style plating. We will show you how to take that store-bought meal and plate it so your family and guests will think you spent hours cooking and preparing it. I will share my philosophy on food, giving you tips and insights on dishes that are uncomplicated yet elegant.

We will showcase a variety of plate shapes, and you can witness their different effects on food presentation. With tricks of the trade, we will help you see how easy it can be to finish a dish and make it look great, no matter how simple the food. This book is both educational and fun. I will share resources with you so you can purchase for your home as the professional chef does. Most of all I want to share my passion for all things culinary and demonstrate how the statement "You eat with your eyes" can come to life for you.

Use this book as a guideline and then let your own creative juices flow while you learn to enjoy working with food. The book is designed to teach, and to share a culinary philosophy that will stir up conversation and produce tasty results.

You Eat with Your Eyes will be a resource book to keep in your library for years to come. Cook with passion, plate with love and creativity, and most of all, have fun!

Big on flavor but small in size, an amuse-bouche is a great way to start off a meal. It allows guests to see your approach to food and to anticipate what is yet to come.

Simplicity and Elegance: the Amuse-Bouche

"Literally meaning to 'entertain the mouth,' amuse-bouche refers to finger food served with drinks."

The keys are simplicity and elegance, a focus on flavor and an eye-appealing presentation. The amuse also gives the guests something to eat with their drinks while waiting for the meal. Creativity is encouraged here: a tasting of one or two bites can showcase an ingredient you want to try or an unusal preparation. Studies show that most people are willing to try new food and flavor concepts in small portions. They may hesitate to order a whole portion or to prepare such a dish in a home setting. However, when served on a cool-looking small plate, an amuse can lead the diner on a culinary journey. Fun and unusual serving plates help enhance presentation and flavor.

Amuse-bouche are limited only by your creativity. Simple flavors let the presentation add to the excitement and allow the freshness of the product to speak loud and clear.

Dinnerware is an important part of the presentation and experience. When serving amuse, the right plates accentuate the food and create the "wow" factor. Little plates, such as those shown here, are widely available today and need only your creativity and food.

When entertaining, an array of small plates along with cocktails lets your guests try many dishes without getting too full. It can be an evening big on taste and lively discussions of food.

Amuse means "to please" in French. These little plates do just that.

To store oysters or clams and maintain the highest quality, fill ziplock bags with crushed ice and place on top of the shellfish while in your refrigerator.

Wellfleet Oysters with Sauce Mignonette

Oysters, they say, are the food of love. In the days of the Roman emperors, oysters cost their weight in gold. Whether they have aphrodisiac powers or not they are still a popular food choice. Oysters also benefit from simplicity in preparation.

One of the finest ways to enhance quality oysters is to serve them cold and raw with a splash of citrus, hot sauce or with a classic mignonette sauce as shown here.

There are many varieties of oysters, however some experts identify three broad classifications: Atlantic (such as Blue Points, Malpeque, and Caraquet), Eastern (such as Wellfleet), and Pacific (Samish Bay, Pearl Bay, and the prized Kumamotos). Oysters can have taste profiles of creamy, salty, mineral and earthy.

The oyster shown here is a Wellfleet served with mignonette sauce, which is simply a quality vinegar such as Champagne or pear along with fresh shallots. What makes this presentation special is the bed of red sea salt it sits on and the square plate that accents the shape of the oyster. It is simple, elegant and tastes good.

Oysters can be poached or broiled, however, there is something special about a high quality oyster, chilled and freshly shucked bought to the plate uncompromised and without modifications.

Wellfleet Oysters
with Sauce
Mignonette

Using an oyster knife, gently open oyster while putting the liquor aside for use later.

Fill plates with red sea salt, tap down on the plate to level the salt in the dish.

Oyster Knife

Designed specifically for opening shellfish, this knife makes a sometimes difficult task fast and easy.

Mignonette Sauce

1 cup red-wine vinegar

1 tbsp freshly ground
  black pepper

1 tbsp minced shallot

• In a small stainless-steel bowl, whisk together all the ingredients. Let the mixture sit for at least 1 day for the flavors to develop.

• When ready to serve, whisk in oyster liquor for added flavor.

Make mignonette sauce by adding minced shallots, oyster liquor and vinegar.

Place oyster on top of salt, spoon mignonette over oyster and serve.

Amuse Bouche

Buying smoked salmon can be confusing with all the varieties and companies available. It can even be ordered on the internet. In my kitchen we make our own. When I buy salmon I look for a nice, quality smoked salmon produced from wild Atlantic or Alaskan salmon.

Potato Blini, Smoked Salmon with Crème Fraîche and Sweet Onion Jam

Whether in Europe or here at home, smoked salmon is considered a delicacy. The ways to serve it are endless and one thing is certain—it is always a favorite. The price can be steep, depending on the type of salmon used and the packaging. Simply put, smoked salmon is a filet that has been cured then hot or cold smoked.

The flavor can vary depending on the cure, the wood used in the smoking and other creative factors as well as the fish itself. Scottish and Irish salmon is considered to be the best along with any smoked salmon made with wild salmon because the flesh offers a natural meaty flavor compared to other, fattier, farm-raised salmon.

Smoked salmon is very popular for canapés and appetizers, is featured at brunches and is usually served with some kind of toast and other accouterments such as sour crème, crème fraîche, onion, capers and egg.

Our version of this amuse plate takes the salty salmon and teams it with a potato blini, crème fraîche and the sweetness of onion jam. It may be only be two bites but it is two bites of heaven with contrasting flavors and textures that almost make the salmon come alive.

The presentation is attractive as the verticality of the salmon above the blini and the quenelle of jam adds an elegant touch.

Potato Blini, Smoked Salmon with Crème Fraîche and Sweet Onion Jam

Spread out the salmon strips and fill with crème fraîche and herbs. Roll salmon in a nice, loose pinwheel and stand up.

Make the blinis using a blini pan. Use butter for great flavor or a cooking spray to reduce the fat.

Silver Dollar Pancake Pan

Making a perfect blini can be difficult but this specialized pancake pan makes it easy to make 7 perfect bite-size blini's.

Potato Blini

2 lbs Yukon gold potatoes

1/4 cup semolina flour

3 to 5 tbsp crème fraîche

1 tbsp extra-virgin olive oil

4 large eggs

2 large egg yolks

• Boil the potatoes in a large pot of salted water. When potatoes are tender, drain them and peel. Pass the potatoes through a ricer.

• Weigh out 1 1/2 pounds of the riced potatoes and place them in a stainless-steel mixing bowl. Whisk the semolina quickly into the potatoes, then whisk in 3 tablespoons of the crème frâiche and the oil. Whisk in the eggs two at a time, whisking until smooth after each addition. Whisk in the yolks. The batter should be the thickness of pancake batter; if it is too thick, whisk in a tablespoon or two more crème fraîche. Use the batter to cook blini as desired.

Take the onion jam and form into a quenelle shape using two spoons.

Place all components on the plate starting with the blini, then the salmon then the onion jam. Notice the contrast of the round shapes against the square plate.

Amuse Bouche

In short, remember that if simply looking at a dish makes you want to eat the food and gives you expectations of something special, you have succeeded.

Roasted Shrimp and Sage with Asian Noodles

Shrimp is everyone's favorite and it lends itself to many preparations. While I enjoy shrimp well poached in a flavorful court bouillon and made into a cocktail, I must say that I don't understand the common practice of boiling shrimp and then sopping them in spicy cocktail sauce that overwhelms the flavor of the shrimp.

Besides being served in a very cool small bowl, our shrimp amuse has a light Asian-style glaze and sits on a small bed of wheat noodles, tossed with some vegetables. The shrimp is wrapped in a sage leaf dipped in butter and a touch of sesame oil then lightly grilled to bring out its sweetness.

The presentation is lovely as the perfectly cooked shrimp wrapped in the sage leaf pops against the background of the whole wheat noodles.

Food presentation can be complex, but in many cases just properly cooked food with big flavors and bright colors will naturally harmonize and look stunning.

Be prepared for guests to ask for seconds of this amuse.

Roasted Shrimp and Sage with Asian Noodles

Take the shrimp and place them in a solution of water and kosher salt for 20 minutes, rinse well, then toss in some extra virgin olive oil, and wrap in a sage leaf.

Grill shrimp for 2-3 minutes on each side and then put aside for a moment. If desired the shrimp may be brushed with a glaze during the grilling to increase flavor.

Asian Vinaigrette

2 tbsp minced scallions

2 tbsp rice-wine vinegar

2 tsp soy sauce

1 tsp minced fresh ginger

1/2 tsp minced garlic

Juice of 1 lemon

1/2 tsp granulated sugar

1/8 tsp freshly ground
  black pepper

1/8 tsp salt

1/3 cup sesame oil

• In a small bowl, whisk together the scallions, rice-wine vinegar, soy sauce, ginger, garlic, sugar, lemon juice, pepper and salt.

• Whisking constantly and pouring in a slow, steady stream, whisk in the sesame oil to form an emulsion.

Place noodles and vegetables in a bowl and toss well with Asian-style dressing. With tongs or a fork twirl a portion of the noodles and place in small bowls.

Top each bed of noodles with shrimp. The shrimp will be highlighted against the contrast of the noodles and specks of color that the vegetables give.

Flavor-rich soup in an espresso cup makes for a great little bite prior to the meal. Or, for a first plate, try three different kinds of soups.

Butternut Squash Soup with Maple Cream and Spice Dust

Soup is universally loved, and why not? A blend of stocks, broths or purees is one of the best foundation foods.

There are three keys to great soup. The first is to use the freshest ingredients possible. The second is proper cooking procedures. Soup needs to be gently simmered and made in stages so the flavors develop properly. The third and final key is simplicity. The soup should feature the flavor of the soup base—all other items should complement the flavor, not mask it. A chicken soup should taste like chicken, not like carrots or onions just because they were used in making the soup.

Fall is one of my favorite times in the kitchen. The season's bounty is filled with great products and flavors to enjoy. Butternut squash, for instance, is a vegetable that has endless uses in the kitchen. From a roasted vegetable for dinner, baked in the oven with maple syrup and butter, to our featured small tasting soup with a touch of maple cream and spice, squash is always enjoyable.

Butternut Squash Soup with Maple Cream and Spice Dust

ISI Dessert Whip

Create custom whipped cream, non-dairy topping, mousse, dressings, mayonnaise and sauces without beating or whisking.

Warm or hot soup should follow the same rule as coffee and always be served in a warm cup. Take the espresso cup and fill with hot water, let sit 1-2 minutes then pour out. Wipe any excess water from the cup.

Use a pitcher or a sauce funnel to ensure the even distribution of the soup and to avoid making a mess on the outside of the cups.

Butternut Squash Soup

2 tbsp unsalted butter

1/2 cup chopped celery

1/2 cup chopped onion

1 tsp chopped garlic

5 cups peeled, seeded, and
   diced butternut squash

1 gallon (16 cups)
   chicken stock

1 tsp ground cinnamon

Salt and freshly ground
   black pepper to taste

- In a large pot, melt the butter over medium-high heat. Add the celery, onion, and garlic and sauté until the vegetables are lightly browned. Add the butternut squash and chicken stock and simmer until the squash is tender.

- Using a slotted spoon, transfer the squash to a blender or food processor and blend with enough liquid to purée. (Work in batches if necessary.) Add more liquid until the soup has the desired consistency.

- Return the soup to the pot and stir in the cinnamon. Taste and season with salt and pepper. Reheat and serve.

Fill ISI gun with flavored cream, add gas cartridge and shake well. Using the gun, place a small amount of the cream on top of the soup.

Using a metal shaker filled with spice mixture, gently shake spice mixture over the cream and serve immediately.

Amuse Bouche

If the brûlée is a bit on the wild side for you, try a spoon or two of risotto with a touch of vanilla bean mixed in and top with the lobster for the same delicious result.

Savory Crème Brûlée, Lobster and Pumpkin Confit

The best thing about an amuse or tasting plate is the adventure. Creating and preparing a unique dish from scratch is the fun part of cooking. Another advantage of an amuse is that people are more apt to try a new dish or combination if it is a small bite or two.

This dish borrows from the pastry kitchen. Crème brûlée, that all-time favorite dessert, turns into a savory base for sweet lobster.

Lobster works well with the flavor of vanilla. The butter poached lobster sits on top of crème brûlée made with lobster cream, a touch of thyme, vanilla bean and shallots.

This unusual dish has a pumpkin confit on the side. Decadence is not just for dessert. This dish is fun, full of flavor and with just two or three bites you will impress your guests prior to the start of a meal. They will be "wowed" by the plate, the food and then, when that first bite is taken, will offer accolades to the cook.

Savory Crème Brûlée, Lobster and Pumpkin Confit

Cooking Torch

The ideal tool for caramelizing sugar on crème brûlée and tarts.

Place desired plates in a small baking dish. Fill plate with custard mixture and fill baking dish with enough warm water to cover dishes by 2/3. The custards are now ready to bake.

Once custards have cooled, cover the top of the custard evenly with sugar. Gently caramelize sugar using a small butane torch.

Savory Custard Base

1 tbsp unsalted butter

1/2 yellow onion, diced

1 tsp minced garlic

1 tsp minced shallot

1/4 cup white wine

4 sprigs fresh thyme

2 cups heavy cream

6 whole large eggs

3 large egg yolks

1 qt whole milk

- In a medium pot over medium heat, melt the butter and cook the onion, garlic, and shallot, stirring, until translucent. Add the wine and thyme and simmer until almost dry. Add the cream, bring to a simmer, and remove from the heat. Discard the thyme.

- In a large bowl, whisk together the eggs and yolks. Pouring in a thin, steady stream and whisking constantly, whisk the hot cream into the eggs. Strain the whole thing through a chinois or fine-mesh strainer, discard the solids, then whisk in the milk.

- Pour the custard mixture into molds, cover the tops with plastic wrap, and cook in a water bath in a 225°F. oven for about 3 hours. Remove from the oven and allow to cool to room temperature; refrigerate if not serving immediately.

Using a small spoon, place the poached lobster on top of the custard.

Place pumpkin confit evenly on one side of plate and serve immediately.

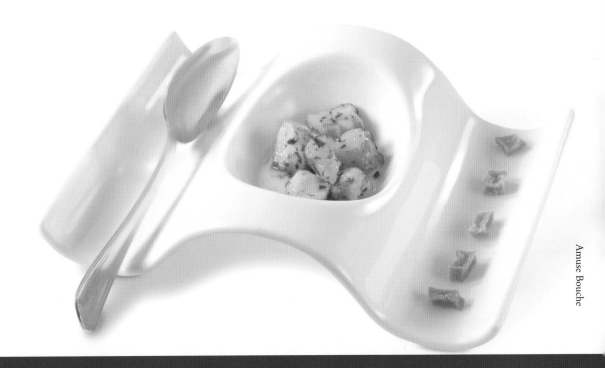

These dishes will give you a culinary template to create and present dishes that have impact from both the presentation and the flavors. Even if you purchase some items to assist you, once you add your own touch and plate the dish with impact, your guests will think you spent all day cooking.

The Impact of First Plates

"The start of the meal sets the tone for what is to come."

The norm for the start of a meal is a salad or cup of soup. There's nothing wrong with either— a signature soup or a composed salad that is more than a bowl of mixed greens can set in motion expectations of what is to come. But you want your guests, whether at a restaurant or at home, to expect a great meal. So why not begin the meal with something that is simple but big on flavor and is presented in a way that makes your guest think, "wow."

The dishes that follow focus on flavor profiles that harmonize and textures that contrast. They use white china that "pops" the food design and/or follows the flow of the food in both shape and design.

Your first plate should take into account the next course or two. Will there be another course or a salad prior to the main plate? Is the main plate on the rich and heavy side? This thinking process will perhaps lead you to start your meal with lighter food, grilled food, a seafood, a vegetarian dish, fruit, or meat.

Before cooking the foie gras, take a small knife, make crisscrosses on the top and chill. Sprinkle with salt, and cook in a heavy bottomed pan on medium heat until nicely browned and caramelized.

Seared Foie Gras, Baked Apple Layers and Red Onion Brûlée

Foie gras is a food that goes back at least to Roman times. It's controversial today, but it's also an item that many top restaurants will not do without. I have a good friend, Rich Rosendale, executive chef at the Greenbrier Resort, whose license plate reads 'Foie Gras.' The man is crazy about foie gras, and his kitchen features it in many ways. It is sinful, it is decadent, it is pleasure, and when prepared properly with accompaniments that complement the richness of the foie, it is a dish to die for.

Foie gras can be purchased in the freezer section of fine food shops already sliced, making it easier for those who cook at home to enjoy. Our version sits on top of baked apple layers with red onion brûlée and apple-port syrup.

The presentation here is on a rectangular plate that contrasts with the round shape of the food in the center—the many, many layers of baked apple, the fat dripping from the foie gras, the rich red of the onion and the spots of syrup. The tart and sweet flavors are in contrast to the richness of the foie gras. This firsst course is sure to get everything off to a great beginning.

Seared Foie Gras, Baked Apple Layers and Red Onion Brûlée

Apple Corer

Raised handles provide leverage while coring and slicing an apple in one quick motion.

Mark the foie with a small knife then pan sear until a rich golden brown.

The center-of-the-plate presentation is highlighted by using a long plate. Place apple in the center of the plate.

Apple Syrup

6 cups apple cider

1 cinnamon stick

1 star anise pod

• In a medium saucepan, combine all the ingredients and bring to a boil over medium-high heat. Boil for 10 minutes, then remove and discard the cinnamon stick and star anise. Continue to boil the cider until it has reduced to a thin syrup (you should have about 1/2 cup), approximately 25 minutes. Cool and store at room temperature.

Place the seared foie gras on the apple, then using two spoons make a quenelle of the red onion brûlée and place on top of the foie gras.

Finish the plate by spooning some cider syrup on each side. Add a touch of sea salt and enjoy.

Don't be intimidated by cook books or recipes—they are guidelines for you to follow. Be creative, cook what you like, and let a picture or book inspire your passion for food, not take it away.

Salad of Carrot, New York Farm Goat Cheese and Honey Dressing

It can be challenging to find first plates that appeal to the tastes of all your guests. Not everyone likes fish; meat can be too heavy; and when people think vegetables, creativity seems to go out the window.

A cook should, however, approach vegetarian food the same way as any food, considering the seasons, textures, flavors, and unique combinations.

The exciting presentation of this dish results from the colors, the different textures of the carrots, and from the flavor bites such as drops of honey, salt, pepper, orange peel, and herbs.

It is another example of how flavor, along with simple techniques, can make a stunning presentation and create dishes that are sure winners to start a meal. And, as with many dishes, they can be served for other parts of the meal as well. This carrot first plate could also be served with grilled raisin bread as a salad course or a light lunch. Sweeten the goat cheese, change some of the flavor bites, place a roasted apple sorbet on the plate, and you could have an interesting dessert course.

This presentation, unlike the foie gras at the center of the plate, is more free form. It uses organic shapes to create a strong and bold image that is sure to get attention.

Salad of Carrot, New York Farm Goat Cheese and Honey Dressing

Take thinly sliced carrots that have been cut lengthways on a mandolin. Fill with softened goat cheese that has been seasoned with some fresh herbs, then roll 3/4 of the way.

Place the carrot rolls around the plate in a freestyle but not sloppy arrangement.

Honey-Thyme Dressing

1/4 cup honey

1/2 cup lemon juice

Leaves from 1 sprig thyme, finely chopped

1 1/4 cups extra-virgin olive oil

Salt and freshly ground black pepper to taste

• In a medium bowl, whisk together the honey, lemon juice, and thyme. Pouring in a slow, steady stream and whisking constantly, whisk in the oil to form an emulsion.

• Taste the dressing and season with salt and pepper.

Position dried carrot slices on the plate then add drops of honey as a dressing.

Finish the plate with edible flowers and seasoned salt, serve with a raisin toast or crostini.

Experiment with drying vegetables, fruits, and herbs. Season the items lightly or brush with some maple syrup. The possibilities are endless; the effects are amazing.

Vegetable Crusted Sea Bass and Vegetable Chips

This dish is an excellent example of visual impact, a dish you truly eat with your eyes. You can appreciate the moist fish, the flavorful juices from the cooking process, and an encrustation of house-made dried vegetables.

The presentation follows the plate—a straight but strong line that is simple and direct. The dried veggies are easy to make. A small investment in a food dehydrator will allow you to create garnishes that not only look nice but also can be eaten. The same process was used for the preceding carrot salad.

Fruits and vegetables can be prepared, sliced, and left in the dehydrator with no supervision. These little flavor bites can be made ahead of time and stored in a sealed container for future use.

Vegetable Crusted
Sea Bass and
Vegetable Chips

Mince dried vegetables for the crust on top of the fish.

Spread a small amount of fish mousse over the fish and apply the dried veggie flakes. The mousse will prevent the flakes from over-cooking.

Fish Mousseline

1 lb fillet of sea bass

1 egg white

1 tbsp shallot, cooked in butter and chilled

1 1/2 tsp kosher salt

1 cup heavy cream

• Remove the bloodline and bones from the fish fillet. Make sure fish is well-chilled, then place it in the bowl of a food processor and pulse 4 to 5 times to begin pureeing the fish. Add the egg white, shallot, and salt. With the motor running, slowly pour the cream in through the feed tube.

• Continue to puree until you have a very smooth mixture. Remove the mousseline from food processor, cover and refrigerate until ready to use.

Place cooked fish on the edge of the plate leaving about three fingers of space from the rim.

Place a variety of whole dried vegetables across from the fish. Finish with some lemon and extra virgin olive oil.

Cutting squares and other shapes means a good bit of fruit left over. Take these pieces, puree them in a blender or processor, then strain overnight though a fine sieve or cheesecloth for cool refreshing fruit water to drink.

Salad of Watermelon, Mango, Goat Cheese, Arugula and Slivered Onions

When we say impact we mean impact, and this salad has it. You may look at it and say, "Well, chef sure uses color in his food." I say in return, "Chef develops his cuisine by flavor first; the colors are the result of foods that work together naturally."

The coolness of watermelon, its sweet taste teamed with squares of mango, the bite of fresh goat cheese, peppery arugula, sweet slivered onions, orange dressing, and a dash of sea salt, all combine with one result— big flavor!

Use a streamlined plating approach along with the food's natural colors and you have a dish that is refreshing and really something special.

Salad of Watermelon, Mango, Goat Cheese, Arugula and Slivered Onions

Mango Pitter

Tropical fruit lovers will appreciate the ease with which this specialty utensil removes a large mango pit, leaving two halves.

Cut and place watermelon rectangles on the plate just a bit off center.

Place mango and watermelon cubes on top of the watermelon base.

Orange Dressing

1 qt orange juice

2 tbsp white-wine vinegar

1 1/2 tsp honey

1/2 cup canola oil

1/4 cup extra-virgin
   olive oil

Salt and freshly ground
   black pepper to taste

• Place the orange juice in a heavy saucepan and bring to a boil. Allow to boil until reduced to 1 cup.

• Place the reduced juice, vinegar, and honey in the bowl of a food processor and process until blended. With the motor running, slowly pour the canola oil and olive oil in through the feed tube to form an emulsion. Taste the dressing and season with salt and pepper.

Top the cubed fruits with the goat cheese, onions and the arugula.

Finish the plate by adding some dressing and the cubed fruit to the left of the plate.

For crisp pastry with distinct layers, bake cold puff pastry in a hot oven. On top of the pastry place a sheet of no-stick paper, then some light pans, to prevent it from rising while it is baking. This is also the secret to a great Napoleon.

Cube of Halibut, Fennel and Red Onion Confit, Butter Pastry and Yellow Curry Emulsion

You may be asking, "Where does chef buy square fish?" Well, fish, of course, are not square. We use a nice thick filet trimmed so it can be cut that way. The trimmings are used for soups and sauces, or perhaps to make a mousse. For home use, purchase a nice center cut from the filet, and then cut the piece into equal portions.

The fish sits on a bed of red onion confit, which in turn sits on a crisp buttery pastry base. The emulsion is extra-virgin olive oil, some yellow pepper purée, and a dash of sweet curry, a totally impactful presentation that has a big flavor profile that will tantalize the palate.

Cube of Halibut, Fennel and Red Onion Confit, Butter Pastry and Yellow Curry Emulsion

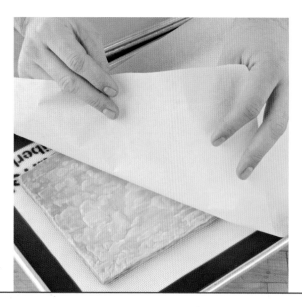

Bake the pastry with extra pans on the top to ensure a crisp product. Once the pastry has cooled, cut into desired shape.

Take the onion confit and spread neatly on the pastry to create a soft bed for the fish.

Red Onion Relish

1 tsp unsalted butter

1 tsp olive oil

2 red onions, slivered

2 tbsp brown sugar

1/2 cup red-wine vinegar

1/2 cup red wine

• In a large sauté pan, heat the butter and oil over medium heat. Add the onions and sugar and sauté until the onions start to caramelize. Add the vinegar and cook until almost completely evaporated. Add the wine and again cook until almost evaporated. Let cool; do not refrigerate.

Place fish on the bed of onions using a fish spatula.

Top the fish with the emulsion by spooning it across the fish in one motion. Top with fresh herbs and sea salt.

If you cannot make the cigars, try the same concept with bought spring rolls or other items you may enjoy serving.

Shrimp Cigars, Asian Slaw and Sweet-n-Sour

Some dishes, like these shrimp cigars, look more complex then they are. The shrimp are laid out with a filling of your choice on brik dough brushed with egg white, then rolled like a cigar. They can be baked or fried.

The presentation, though effective, is simple, using a rectangular dish with some slight depth. The cigars are nestled on a bed of Asian-style slaw that fills three quarters of the dish. This leaves a nice space for the sauce without adding another serving vessel.

Good presentations should be sensible as well as exciting looking. Served in this manner, the sauce adds depth and color to the dish while making it easy to dip the cigars in and mix with the slaw.

The cigars are brushed lightly with some sauce and topped with black and white sesame seeds.

Shrimp Cigars, Asian Slaw and Sweet-n-Sour

Toss the slaw with some rice vinegar and sesame oil then put on the plate and press down covering 3/4 of the surface.

Spoon sauce into open section of plate until the sauce reaches the height of the slaw.

Asian Style Slaw

1 head savoy cabbage,
  sliced thinly

1 small red onion, sliced

1 bunch large scallions,
  trimmed and thinly sliced

1/4 cup soy sauce

1/4 cup vegetable oil

2 tbsp lemon juice

1 tbsp grated fresh ginger

1 tbsp rice vinegar

1 tbsp dark-brown sugar

1 tsp Asian sesame oil

1 tsp salt

Freshly ground black
  pepper to taste

- Toss the cabbage, onion, and scallions together in a large bowl until thoroughly mixed.

- In a small bowl, whisk together the soy sauce, vegetable oil, lemon juice, ginger, vinegar, brown sugar, sesame oil, and salt. Pour the mixture over the cabbage and toss to coat. Season with pepper to taste. Serve the slaw within 1 hour of mixing it or it will become limp and soggy.

Place the shrimp cigars on a slight bias evenly over the slaw.

Brush some sauce or oil on the cigars and sprinkle with the sesame seeds.

Because many vegetables are neutral in flavor, you can add meat, fish, other proteins, and combinations from the global pantry for big taste and a filling, complete meal.

Culinary Poetry with Salads

"As a meal, as a snack, or as part of the menu, salads mean that freshness and flavors abound."

Salads are a favorite, whether at home, at restaurants, or even on the fast food scene. Some of this popularity comes from the perception that eating a salad means eating healthily. Salads can be healthful, depending on the ingredients and, most of all, on the dressing. Add a tantalizing presentation, and your salad will be complete.

The key is to use the freshest ingredients and prepare them in a way that respects the product and highlights the flavors. From the point of view of presentation alone, salads can be a sure winner, with vibrant colors, sparkling dressings, fresh herbs, and ingredients with superb flavor profiles.

Salads are not meant for serving only in bowls. Deep bowls can hide all the beauty. The salads here are picturesquely plated on shallow bowls, square plates, and flat plates with intriguing shapes. A few are new spins on classics such as Caesar salad and Cobb salad, but all are practical and simple and depend on seasonal fare.

Making salads using products that are in season adds to their appeal, their flavor, and even the presentation. A summer tomato is, hands down, more beautiful and flavorful than a tomato in the winter.

Instead of using cold bacon bits, for the best flavor and texture, cook your bacon or pancetta just prior to serving your salad. Pancetta has more spice and really adds spark to your salads.

Cosette's Cobb Salad

Cobb salad is a traditional favorite that has stood the test of time. I love the challenge of taking such a dish and using it as a foundation for something new and perhaps improved, depending on your point of view.

My daughter Cosette, who was named for a character in the French novel Les Misérables, has always had her own opinions about food. She ate foie gras at three years of age and has a passion for what she calls "stinky cheese." Present a nice Stilton or blue, and she is in heaven. She helped me dredge raw chicken breasts in the kitchen at five years of age, and because she helped me roll out and cook my famous meatball recipe when she was six she has named them "Cosette's meatballs." I named this salad after her because it incorporates many of her favorite foods: raspberries, shrimp, egg, chicken, avocado, and pancetta.

It places a new spin on an old favorite and has become a best seller on my menus. It has diverse textures and a variety of flavors that say, "Spring is here." It is one of those salads that can also be a light dinner that satisfies on hot summer nights.

Cosette's Cobb Salad

Metal Spatula

This kitchen utensil is used for multiple purposes, depending on the shape, size and material of the spatula. Metal spatulas are most often made for lifting, turning, serving, and spreading food toppings but also can used to separate food.

Lightly toss chopped iceberg and romaine lettuce with olive oil, salt and pepper. Place seasoned lettuce in bottom of salad bowl.

Using a straight edge as a guide, arrange all garnishes on top of lettuce in straight lines.

Ranch Dressing

2 cups mayonnaise

2 cups buttermilk

1 cup sour cream

1 bunch fresh chives, chopped

2 tbsp chopped parsley

1 tsp onion powder

1 tsp garlic salt

1/2 tsp freshly ground black pepper

1/2 tsp kosher salt

• Place all the ingredients in a stainless-steel bowl and whisk until well combined. Refrigerate overnight to allow the flavors to blend before using.

Place your favorite dressing into a squeeze bottle and lightly drizzle over the salad. Serve extra dressing on the side if desired.

Place a piece of pancetta that you crisped in the oven on top to add flavor as well as texture.

For a Caesar that is special, do not skimp on quality. Use the finest ingredients: imported anchovies, real Parmigiano Reggiano cheese, and dressing you've made yourself. With a blender, it is quick and easy.

A New Kind of Caesar

Caesar salad, featured on the menus of both fine dining restaurants and fast-food chains, is probably the most popular salad available. This Caesar is done just a little differently to add some visual excitement to the dish. The romaine can be washed hours ahead and sliced only when it's time to serve. The slice of romaine with Caesar dressing sits on top of two large Parmesan breadsticks made with puff pastry.

You can, of course, buy breadsticks rather than make them. If you do, make sure you purchase ones of quality. You can also take a slice of semolina bread and lightly grill the bread with extra-virgin olive oil and use that as your base.

After that, add some anchovies, some dollops of dressing, and a Parmesan cookie and you are ready to impress your guests with a new kind of Caesar.

A New Kind
of Caesar

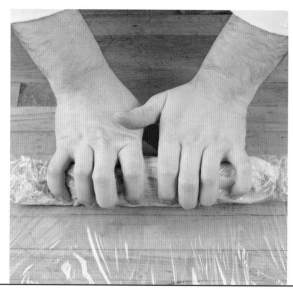

While holding romaine upright, drizzle Caesar dressing evenly in between leaves.

Place dressed romaine on a sheet of plastic wrap. Wrap romaine tightly with plastic and place in refrigerator for 30 minutes to set.

Low Fat Caesar Dressing

1/2 cup low-fat mayonnaise

1/2 cup no-fat Greek-style
yogurt

1/4 cup finely grated
Parmigiano-Reggiano
cheese

1 tbsp lemon juice

1/2 tsp Worcestershire sauce

1 clove garlic, minced

2 tsp minced white
anchovies

1/4 tsp kosher salt

1/8 tsp freshly ground
black pepper

• In a medium bowl, whisk together all the ingredients until well blended. If too thick, whisk in water a little at a time.

Place 2 bread sticks on each plate. Slice wrapped romaine into 3 inch thick pieces, unwrap from the plastic wrap and place on top of bread sticks.

Top romaine with parmesan crisp. Use rolled anchovies filets and remaining dressing to finish plate.

Giancarlo's, "Yes, I am a Vegetarian" Salad

I recall the day some years ago when a waiter came into the kitchen and said, "I've got a vegetarian customer, chef. What can you do?" The immediate response was to dish up a plate of whatever vegetables were being served that evening and send it on its way.

As my cuisine developed, I came to believe strongly that no matter what people might choose to eat, it should be the best. If they want macaroni and cheese, then so be it. Make a damn good macaroni and cheese, one that they will remember. The same applies to vegetarian meals. Why should they not be every bit as good as the other food—creative, with interesting textures and big flavors?

My son Giancarlo, who is seven and keeps near his bed a copy of the vegetarian pledge never to hurt animals, has inspired me even more. He has given me a new respect for those who do not eat meat.

This salad combines crisp toast, creamy cheese topped with fresh and homemade dried vegetables, asparagus spears, asparagus ribbons and roasted sweet cippollini onions.

Giancarlo's,
"Yes I am a
Vegetarian" Salad

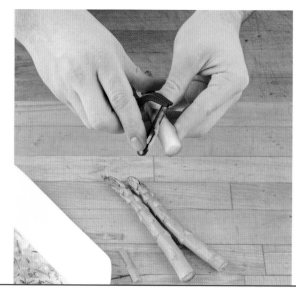

Peeler

*Not your old peeler, today's
peelers enhance almost every
dish with slender, uniform
strips of fruits and vegetables,
citrus peel, even chocolate.*

Using a small knife, gently cut around the end of a
piece of jumbo asparagus approximately 2 inches
from bottom. Be careful not to cut too deeply.

Using a peeler, gently peel the end of asparagus up to
where you scored it with knife. This creates a very
clean look.

Tomato Dressing

1 1/2 cups strained
   tomatoes or tomato purée
1 cup extra-virgin olive oil
1/4 cup balsamic vinegar
1/2 cup chopped fresh basil
Kosher salt and freshly
   ground black pepper
   to taste

• Combine the tomatoes, oil, vinegar, and basil in a blender and blend
until smooth. Taste the dressing and season with salt and pepper.

Using a mandolin, carefully slice an asparagus lengthwise into thin strips. Lightly toss strips with dressing. Wrap asparagus strips around cippolini onions and place to the side.

Place garnished flat bread off to one side of plate. Place dressed mixed greens directly above flat bread. Alternately place two pieces of peeled asparagus. Top asparagus spears with wrapped cippolinis and drizzle with remaining dressing.

The little spice stencil in the corner is not just there for decoration but also to add some flavor to a dish done in a unique way.

Salads of the Land and Sea

People enjoy choices, especially Americans. Even coffee houses have to offer a latte six different ways to please the customer. In Europe this is not so much the case. Menus are presented in seasonal fashion, featuring what is indigenous to the area at that time of year.

You might have a choice of Coke, Diet Coke, or water, not eight different flavors of soft drinks. Coffee houses offer espresso and cappuccino of good quality, and perhaps decaf, but that is all.

In cooking, many people like the opportunity to sample several different ingredients on a plate. Why just have filet mignon when you can get the filet and shrimp as well? That is the direction of this salad. It teams up two favorites: shrimp salad and chicken salad, both served in tomatoes. The chicken salad has been enhanced with diced figs, while the shrimp salad gets a hint of vanilla in the dressing

Salads of the Land and Sea

Using a small knife, cut tomato in half using alternating cuts to create a crown effect. Scoop out the tomato center and fill one half of tomato with shrimp salad and the other half with chicken salad. Place both stuffed tomatoes on plate.

Using a small knife, cut prepared asparagus in half lengthwise. Arrange alternately in center of plate between the stuffed tomatoes.

ECL Chicken Salad

2 cups diced grilled skinless
chicken breast

4 dried figs, plumped in hot
apple juice and thinly slice

1 apple, shredded

1 1/4 cups mayonnaise

1/4 cup extra-virgin
olive oil

Juice of 1 lime

2 tsp Spice de Cosette
seasoning

2 tsp minced tarragon

Kosher salt and ground
black pepper to taste

• Mix all the ingredients except the salt and pepper together in a large bowl. Taste the salad and season with salt and pepper to taste.

Using a small stencil as a guide, gently shake spice mixture on plate to form a design.

Finish plate with a drizzle of vinaigrette and picked herbs.

When seasoning a dressing or vinaigrette with salt, pepper, or herbs, add these seasonings first to the vinegar or juice to dissolve and develop flavors. Many of these will not dissolve as well in the oil.

Composed Vegetable Salad Pouch with Tomato Jam and Lemon Honey Citrus Dressing

This salad is pure poetry—flavorful vegetables all wrapped up in a pouch. Marinating gives the vegetables additional flavor. The practical, yet different, presentation creates visual impact.

You can choose any vegetable salad or mix of vegetables you desire. For a fusion of different flavors and textures, try making a salad that incorporates roasted vegetables, grilled vegetables, and blanched vegetables. Dressing is as essential to a salad as sauces are to a meal.

Keeping in mind that freshness is key, try to think in new directions. A juice machine can create a variety of interesting and very fresh dressings—try a ginger and carrot dressing or apple-carrot vinaigrette. Using two parts of fresh juice, one part of a neutral oil, and one part vinegar is a good way to start. For low fat dressings, forget the oil, and go with three parts juice to one part vinegar, and then whisk in one or two tablespoons of quality oil. You may need to thicken the juice slightly with a slurry of cornstarch to create a oil-like consistency. Add one tablespoon of starch to two tablespoons of liquid; bring the juice to a boil, then whisk in the slurry and simmer three to four minutes. Let it cool, and then make your dressing.

Composed Vegetable Salad Pouch with Tomato Jam and Lemon Honey Citrus Dressing

Squeeze Bottle

Available in various sizes, this simple tool is great at delivering sauces and dressings in specific places.

Place a soft rice paper on a sheet of plastic wrap. Place dressed salad mixture in center of rice paper. Gather all corners of plastic wrap to form rice paper in a ball around salad mix. Place in refrigerator for 20 minutes to set.

Remove plastic wrap and place wrapped salad in center of plate. Arrange vegetable garnish around wrapped salad.

Tomato-Fennel Jam

1 cup apple-cider vinegar

3/4 cup brown sugar

2 packets unflavored gelatin

1/2 cup citron vodka

3 pounds ripe Roma
  tomatoes, peeled and
  chopped

1 cup thinly sliced fennel

1 tbsp grated orange zest

1/2 tsp ground cloves

1 vanilla bean, cut into
  4 pieces

1 tsp red-pepper flakes

Salt to taste

• In a bowl, stir together the vinegar, sugar, gelatin, and vodka, stirring until the sugar dissolves. Transfer the mixture to a heavy stainless-steel 5-quart saucepan and stir in all the remaining ingredients except the salt. Bring the mixture to a boil over high heat. Reduce heat to medium and simmer, stirring occasionally, until most of the liquid has evaporated, 35 to 40 minutes.

• Remove from the heat and let cool for 1 hour. Season to taste with salt, then refrigerate until chilled.

Using two small spoons, form tomato jam into quenelle shape. Place quenelle on top of wrapped salad.

Using a squeeze bottle, drizzle extra dressing around plate. Sprinkle wrapped salad with sea salt and cracked black pepper.

This plate is carpaccio-style, in which an item is sliced very thin and used to line the plate as a foundation for the other food items. You could use tomato, mango, even traditional beef filet for a unique twist on this dish.

Chef Leonard's Duet of Lobster and Papaya

Lobster is an all-American favorite, but most cooks do not realize that this great crustacean pairs well with combinations of fruits such as mango and papaya.

This unique duo creates its own poetry from the natural colors, flavor profiles and the use of a bowl that accents the presentation.

When possible, use fresh lobster meat. It is worth the expense and the effort. This salad combines the sweetness of the lobster, the peppery touch of the frisee, the juicy bite of the tomatoes, all brought together by slices of papaya. Finish with a nice Champagne or citrus vinaigrette, and the poem reads, "Savor each bite. Enjoy the culinary ecstasy."

Chef Leonard's Duet of Lobster and Papaya

Mandolin

This classic chef's tool is used to slice foods in varying thicknesses and shapes, including straight, wavy, crinkled and julienne.

Using a mandolin, thinly slice a peeled piece of papaya. Fan slices of papaya 3/4 of the way around bowl, making sure to overlap the previous piece of papaya with the next.

Place a small amount of mixed greens that have been lightly tossed with dressing into the center of the plate.

Papaya Vinaigrette

1/4 cup papaya purée or
    nectar
1 tbsp shallot, minced
1/4 cup champagne vinegar
1 tsp fresh mint
Salt and pepper to taste
1/2 cup extra-virgin
    olive oil

• In a small bowl, whisk together the papaya purée or nectar, shallot, vinegar, mint and salt and pepper.

• While whisking slowly add the olive oil to form an emulsified dressing. This dressing may be made a few days in advance and stored in the refrigerator until ready to use.

Toss lobster meat and peeled tomatoes lightly in dressing. Place marinated lobster and tomatoes on top of salad.

Entertaining at home at lunchtime can be a pleasure. Prep a few items ahead. When the time comes, put together your own lunch dishes, dishes that will stir the senses and make for an enjoyable time for you and your guests.

Creating Visual Interest with Lunch

"Not just a sandwich anymore, not just a bite on the run, but great food with high style and endless flavor."

Many would say lunch is not as important as breakfast, but it is nevertheless an important meal that serves many purposes—business meetings, social events, a daily break from the job, or an opportunity for friends to get together to catch up. Lunch can be grab-and-go, quick and on the run, but many people want to take time to stop and smell the food.

Lunch can be a dinner-type meal with smaller portions. It can be salad enhanced by adding proteins and vegetables. It can be an elegant modern creation like our open-faced lobster sandwich.

Whatever the purpose, like all meals, it should be special. The presentation of lunch food should whet the appetite, stir the senses, and ensure that a meal with a time limit is still one to remember.

Food cooked properly and presented in a clean manner creates interest. Sitting in a restaurant and seeing the person next to you served our featured maple salmon or pancetta cod, you would immediately ask yourself, "Do I really want that turkey on rye?" No, you would want to explore the menu. The beautifully presented dish tells you, "Indulge, go for it, eat well, give your appetite a treat."

Baby spinach would work well, but don't fry it. For better flavor and better digestion, just toss it with a warm dressing to wilt the spinach.

Torte of Portobello, Tomato, Mozzarella and Fried Spinach

"Torte" is difficult to define in today's world where menu terminology runs wild. It traditionally means a rich cake made with little or no flour then filled with butter icing, chocolate, jam, or whipped cream. Today, the word "torte" is also used to mean layers of anything—vegetables, pasta, and the like.

The name has a nice ring to it—it sounds like something you *want* to eat—so in the interest of effective marketing, we might forgive a little looseness in terminology. One could argue that this lunch dish is far better called a torte than a skewer.

Choosing the layers of flavor is up to you. This dish combines meaty and good-tasting grilled portobello mushrooms with two other favorites, fresh mozzarella and tomato. The unique part is the fried spinach salad and dried tomatoes. The torte is laced with a pesto dressing that is low in fat and tart with acid to cut the oliness from the fried spinach.

Torte of Portobello, Tomato, Mozzarella, and Fried Spinach

Metal Picks

Substantial metal picks easily pierce harder foods and add a sleek sophisticated look.

Place 2 grilled portobello mushrooms on work surface. Using a round cutter, trim the mushrooms to make them the same size.

Lay one mushroom upside down on work service. Place a slice of tomato on top and season with salt and pepper. Place sliced fresh mozzarella on top of tomato and season. Place a second layer of tomato on top of mozzarella followed by the other mushroom.

Dried Tomato Chips

1 tsp granulated sugar

1/2 tsp freshly ground
    black pepper

1 tsp kosher salt

2 each firm plum tomatoes

• In a small bowl, combine the sugar, pepper and salt and set aside.

• Using a mandolin or slicing machine, slice the plum tomatoes into strips about 1/8-inch thick. Lay the strips on a sheet pan lined with a silicone baking mat and sprinkle them with the sugar mixture.

• Dry the slices in a 200°F. oven for about 2 hours. Once dried, gently remove the tomato chips from the baking mat and place them in an airtight container between sheets of wax paper until ready to use.

Insert four medal skewers into mushroom torte. Using a serrated knife cut torte into 4 equal pieces. Lay torte sections on plate leaving room in the center.

Spoon dressing over each piece of the torte. Fill center of plate with the fried spinach and top with tomato crisp.

This salad is also versatile. For a low fat salad, grilled chicken breast or poached shrimp can be used. If you are a vegetarian, try topping this salad with a portobello mushroom cap hot off the grill.

The Best Damn Steak Salad

Salads should be more than lettuce or greens in a bowl with vegetables and cold meat or fish. Yes, salads can be a symphony of vegetables and fruits, different flavors and textures, topped with a piece of fresh-cooked protein that turns the plate into a complete meal and a delicious one.

This salad is a natural—beets, apples, and French green beans served with goat cheese fritters, an apple-Champagne dressing, and a hot-off-the-grill flatiron steak. It's a meal that has an enormous impact in both flavor and visual presentation. The flavor contrasts are amazing—the roasted beets, sautéed French green beans that have a crisp snap, sweet and tart apples, a fried fritter with creamy goat cheese, and finally a lively dressing with a foundation of pure apple cider and Champagne.

Trust me, there is nothing more you could want from this dish, except to enjoy the pleasures it will bring you and your guests.

The Best Damn Steak Salad

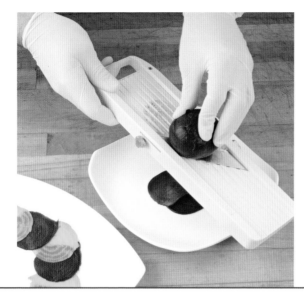 

Using a mandolin, slice beets into thin slices. Overlap slices around plate to form base, being sure to alternate colors.

Place marinated haricots verts in center of beets. Using an alligator chopper, dice an apple and add the apples cubes around the outside of the haricots verts.

Alligator Chopper

With one quick press, hinged plastic cutters slice food into "sticks" with a razor-sharp grid of stainless blades. Turn "sticks," then press again for "cubes."

Warm Goat Cheese Fritters

10.5 oz plain or herbed
  goat cheese (1 log)

2 extra-large egg whites,
  beaten

3 cups fresh white
  bread crumbs

1 tbsp olive oil

1 tbsp unsalted butter

Kosher salt to taste

• Using a piece of dental floss, slice the Goat cheese into 12, 1/2-inch-thick slices. Dip each slice into the beaten egg whites, then the bread crumbs, being sure the cheese is thoroughly coated. Place the slices on a rack and chill for at least 15 minutes in the refrigerator.

• Melt oil and butter in a sauté pan over medium-high heat until butter begins to bubble. Cook the goat cheese rounds quickly on both sides until browned on the outside but not melted inside. Remove from the pan and place into a paper towel and salt lightly, serve immediately.

Lay slices of sliced steak over haricots verts.
When laying slices of steak, alternate direction to
build height.

Place cheese fritters around center salad. Finish plate
with a drizzle of dressing, sea salt and fresh herbs.

When preparing lobster for this dish, lobster rolls, or pasta, remember that the effort of cooking fresh lobster and taking it out of the shell is always worth it. There's a huge difference between freshly cooked lobster and the frozen or cooked-to-death fresh lobster meat sold in stores.

Open-faced Lobster Sandwich,
Salad of Cauliflower and Potato

Maine lobster, sweet Maine lobster, is my favorite indulgence. Though many chefs love foie gras, I love lobster, and during the season I feature this incredible item on my menus in various ways.

Treated with respect and prepared with thought, a complex yet sophisticated lobster preparation can bring much more to the table than a lobster that is merely boiled or thrown into the oven with a bunch of bread stuffing.

This dish, besides creating visual impact, follows one of my most important rules of flavor: always create layers of flavor (lobster and cauliflower are as natural a match as truffle and potato). This salad has diced Yukon gold potatoes, a touch of truffle oil, homemade mayonnaise, and roasted cauliflower. Your palate will thank you for the experience.

The lobster tails are poached gently in butter and then sliced. Placed on toasted bread, they unite for a true marriage of flavors.

Open Faced
Lobster Sandwich,
Salad of
Cauliflower and
Potato

Place potato and cauliflower salad evenly on two pieces of flat bread. Place flat breads on plate at a slight angle.

Using a very sharp knife, slice lobster tail into even slices on a bias to create a larger slice perception.

Cauliflower Potato Salad

2 tbsp peanut butter

2 tbsp white truffle oil

1/2 cup mayonnaise

Salt and pepper to taste

2 cups diced and cooked
   Yukon gold potatoes

3 celery ribs peeled,
   chopped fine

1/4 cup chopped thyme

3 hard-cooked eggs,
   chopped

1 cup cooked cauliflower
   florets

Shaved fresh truffle

• Whisk the peanut butter, truffle oil and the mayonnaise in a small bowl until smooth. Season with salt and pepper

• Put the potatoes, celery, thyme and egg in a bowl, add the cauliflower. Fold in the dressing with the potatoes and cauliflower.

• Let sit in the refrigerator for at least 2 hours for flavors to develop. Shave fresh truffle over salad if desired, serve at room temperature

Shingle slices of lobster over potato and cauliflower salad.

Lightly drizzle vinaigrette over lobster meat. Finish plate with a sprinkle of red sea salt and fresh-picked thyme.

You can make great soups such as this one can easily by simmering your main ingredient in broth with aromatics and herbs then finish in a blender until smooth, making a healthy meal.

Portobello Soup, Sage Cream, Portobello Chips and Extra Virgin Olive Oil

Soups are a good way to judge if someone knows how to cook. Soups are a true example of developing layers of flavor that finally come together for something very special.

Soups can be accented with many flavor bites such as butters, herbs, flavored oils, creams, vegetables and other garnishes that accentuate the final product.

Our mushroom soup is not only elegant, but big on flavor. The bowl I've used is really off-beat and will entice your guests as soon as they see it. The edges of the plate can be used for a variety of chips, your soup spoon, crackers, or just slices of bread.

Portobello Soup, Sage Cream, Portobello Chips and Extra Virgin Olive Oil

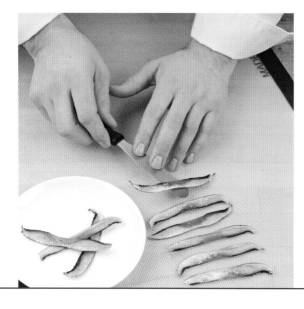

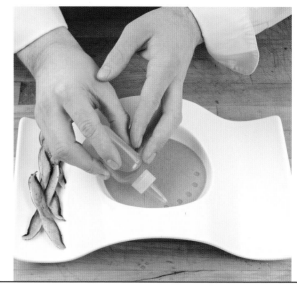

Milk Frother

You can froth freely with this handy device dedicated to perfect foamed milk, as well as foam garnishes.

Carefully remove dried mushrooms from Silpat (a brand of non-stick silicone mat) and set aside.

Place soup into warm bowl. Overlap dried mushrooms along one side of plate. Using a small squeeze bottle, place drops of oil around edge of soup.

Portabello Chips

1 tsp granulated sugar

1/2 tsp freshly ground
  black pepper

1 tsp kosher salt

2 fresh portobello
  mushroom caps

• In a small bowl, combine the sugar, pepper and salt and set aside.

• Using a small spoon, gently remove the gills from the underside of the mushroom caps. Using a sharp knife, slice the caps into strips about 1/8-inch thick. Lay the strips on a sheet pan covered with a silicone baking mat and sprinkle them with the sugar mixture.

• Dry the slices in a 200°F. oven for about 2 hours. Once dried, gently remove the mushroom chips from the baking mat and place them in an airtight container between sheets of wax paper until ready to use.

Place tarragon foam into a small bowl. Froth foam using a milk frother to create the foam effect

Spoon tarragon foam into the center of the soup and serve immediately.

Take a few minutes to cut your vegetables into different shapes and the results are dramatic even for the simplest of vegetables.

Salisbury Steak Chop, Olive Oil Mashed Potatoes, Garden Vegetables and Mushroom Jus Lie

Okay, I cannot resist taking an old favorite comfort food and putting a new spin on it. Salisbury steak is a diner and comfort-food classic—a combo of ground beef patty with vegetables, roasted in the oven, served with gravy and potatoes, preferably mashed.

My version is not that different, except that I use a mix of quality ground beef shoulder and some ground pork with sautéed onions, garlic, and carrots. Toss in some spices, condiments, and a binding agent, and away we go. I shape our Salisbury steak almost like a large pork chop, and then use a roasted white asparagus to suggest the bone.

We now have a rustic lunch dish with elegant visual interest—a comfort-food meat dish combined with nicely cut vegetables, a shaped portion of mashed potatoes and rich gravy.

Salisbury Steak Chop, Olive Oil Mashed Potatoes, Garden Vegetables and Mushroom Jus Lie

Using a white asparagus as a "bone", begin to form the chop by wrapping meat mixture around the asparagus.

Place meat on work service and finish shaping the meat to form a "chop". Cook chops on a grill to the desired doneness.

Simply The Best Mashed Potatoes

1 1/2 lbs Yukon gold potatoes

1 tbsp kosher salt, or as needed

1/2 cup heavy cream

1/2 cup milk

8 oz high-quality unsalted butter, diced

Sea salt and ground white pepper to taste

• Scrub the potatoes well but do not peel them. Place them in a large stainless-steel saucepan and add cold spring water and to cover the potatoes by about 2 inches. Add 1 tbsp of kosher salt per every quart of water used. Bring to a boil, lower the heat to medium and simmer until the potatoes are tender. Drain.

• In a saucepan, combine the cream and milk and bring to a boil; remove from the heat and set aside.

• Peel the potatoes and cut them into pieces. Pass them through a ricer twice and then place them in a heavy stainless-steel saucepan. Place over low heat and stir vigorously with a wooden spoon for 3 to 5 minutes. Add a little of the butter at a time, stirring until the butter is incorporated and the potatoes are fluffy. Slowly stir in the cream mixture. Taste the potatoes and season with salt and a touch of white pepper.

Place a quenelle of potato puree onto plate. Spoon the sautéed vegetables onto the plate next to the potatoes. Lean the cooked chop against the potatoes.

Gently spoon sauce onto the chop allowing the sauce to flow onto the plate. Finish plate with a bit of sea salt and serve.

Lunch

Pancetta infuses the fish with flavor while keeping it moist during the baking process. It also adds a slightly crisp texture but does not overpower the sweet meatiness of the cod.

Pancetta Cod, Bed of Zucchini, Carrot Emulsion, Carrot Flakes and Cube of Yellow Carrots

Today, fish has become the protein of choice for many reasons, but mostly because people see it as being healthier than other proteins. Fish can be healthy, but anyone who knows and understands food realizes that all food is both good and bad and in moderation most proteins have benefits.

For maximum freshness, fish should be stored at 36 degrees and sold within 48 hours. If you then handle it carefully, cook it until it is just done, and dress it up properly with flavors and color in mind, it will become the star of the plate.

Our cod, sitting on a bed of zucchini ribbons, is flavored by thin slices of pancetta and finished with heirloom carrots presented three ways. Visual interest, yes; flavor interest, just incredible.

Pancetta Cod, Bed of Zucchini, Carrot Emulsion, Carrot Flakes and Cube of Yellow Carrots

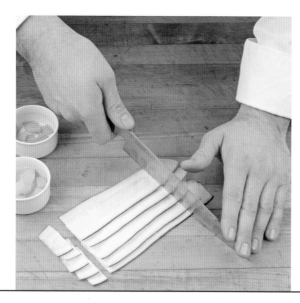

Shingle thin strips of zucchini on a cutting board. Using a knife cut zucchini to desired length. Place zucchini on a serving plate and season with extra virgin olive oil, salt and pepper.

Using a spoon or spatula, gently place emulsion to one side of zucchini to complement the shape of zucchini. Place a few carrot chips on top of emulsion.

Chef's Turner

This versatile kitchen tool easily slips under foods. It's ideal for fish, but you'll find it helpful whenever you want to flip something.

Carrot Emulsion

2 soft-boiled eggs, shelled

1/4 cup diced
    cooked carrot

1/4 cup apple cider

1/4 tsp minced fresh ginger

1/3 cup extra-virgin
    olive oil

2 tbsp blanched mint
    leaves

4 to 8 tbsp carrot juice

Sea salt to taste

• In a blender, combine the eggs, carrot, cider, and ginger and blend on high until smooth. With the motor running, slowly pour in the oil. Add the mint and purée.

• Strain the mixture into a bowl and whisk in carrot juice until the mixture is the proper consistency. Taste and season the emulsion with sea salt.

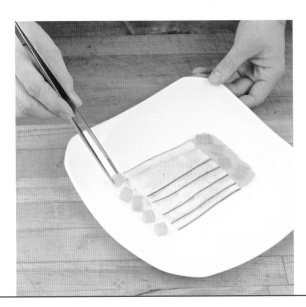 

Place glazed carrot cubes in a straight line on the opposite side of the emulsion.

Place pancetta wrapped cod in center of zucchini base and serve immediately.

How you present food is, of course, important. We do eat with our eyes. Over the years, I have observed that people think a dish was far better than it actually was because the presentation was so appealing.

Layers of Flavor with Main Plates

"The star of the dinner, radiant with the season's bounty, a middle course cooked with passion to keep the table conversation going."

This section will focus on main plates, or "entrées", that are usually served at dinner. What we strive for in main plates is the creation of layers of flavor, and we plate the food to emphasize it.

"Layers of flavor" does not mean stacking food in a tall, awkward pile. It means layering flavors of food by using different cooking techniques, different textures, and different ingredients that harmonize, even though each one seems to be given star treatment. It also means, as with all dishes, giving thought to the shape, color, and china selection

Even a simple dish such as pasta can have layers of flavor that engage the appetite as well as bring the eye to the plate. Many chefs spend time designing food on a plate so that its beauty will "wow" the diner. They neglect, however, the simple magic of food cooked well, with colors and flavors all coming together. For me, the flavors should to speak for themselves, so my canvas needs to be simple, yet elegant and stylish. The plating should give the dish punch, but it should always respect the real star—the food itself.

For the best risotto, use the Vialone Nano or the Carnaroli varieties rather than the much-marketed and more commercial Arborio rice.

Black Risotto, Framed Sweet Nantucket Scallops and Crispy Calamari

Yes, this is a striking dish, but you may be wondering, "What is the black in that risotto?" The black is fresh squid ink, often used to color pasta, rice, and other items. It does taste a bit fishy, but used in the right amounts, it adds dramatic color in a natural way while complementing the fish with its slight salty, earthy tang.

The key here is to use the right amount. Aside from its abundant layers of flavor, what makes this dish special is the simple but very effective presentation.

The risotto, creamy and earthy, complemented by sweet, just-cooked scallops, contrasts with the texture and flavor of crisp calamari. This dish is then framed with white asparagus and a bit of shrimp sauce for a meal that will delight the senses in every way.

The best part is that it is far easier to prepare than it looks.

Black Risotto, Framed Sweet Nantucket Scallops and Crispy Calamari

Place the risotto in a ring mold and press lightly then remove the mold.

Place the four asparagus like a box on top of the risotto.

Seasoned Flour

4 cups all-purpose flour

3 cups cornstarch

2 tbsp kosher salt

1 tsp paprika

1 tsp ground white pepper

1 tsp Old Bay seasoning

1/2 tsp cayenne

1/2 tsp granulated garlic

• Mix all the ingredients together in a medium mixing bowl until well combined. Can be made up to a week ahead and stored in an airtight container.

Place the scallops in the center of the
asparagus frame.

Top the scallops with the fried calamari and finish
with some sauce on the four corners.

Even a meal such as this can be easy. Vegetables can be diced the day before; the meat can be pre-seared and ready for the oven; the potatoes, partially cooked and roasted before service.

Loin of American-Raised Lamb, Roasted Potatoes, Eggplant Chips, Ratatouille and Rich Lamb Jus

Lamb is the "other red meat", and for a long time it has received too much negative press. The flavor and the nutritional benefits have come a long way. American-raised lambs are fed a combination of mixed grains and mixed grasses; this feed contributes to a milder flavor and less gamey texture then many people expect.

A three- to four-ounce portion of lean lamb has fewer than 230 calories and many vitamins and minerals.

Most importantly, it tastes great, and the many different cuts lend themselves to a great variety of dishes.

This dish is full of those layers of flavor—nicely roasted loin, potatoes roasted in olive oil, fried basil, and ratatouille, a natural accompaniment. The potatoes act as a base, or a socle, to raise the lamb and give the dish height for a clean and effective presentation. Top it with some eggplant chips and a sauce, and you are ready to enjoy something special.

Loin of American-Raised Lamb, Roasted Potatoes, Eggplant Chips, Ratatouille and Rich Lamb Jus

Layer the sliced roasted potatoes on the plate in a curve.

Place the ratatouille to the right of the last potato and towards the first.

30-Minute Ratatouille

1/4 cup extra-virgin olive oil

1 small sweet onion, finely diced

3 cloves garlic, thinly sliced

2 zucchini, diced

1 yellow squash, diced

2 red bell peppers, diced

1 small firm Italian eggplant, cubed

3 sprigs fresh oregano

5 ripe Roma tomatoes, peeled, seeded, and diced

3/4 cup strained canned Italian tomatoes

Salt and red pepper flakes to taste

• Preheat the oven to 450°F. Heat the oil in a large, heavy, ovenproof pot over medium-high heat. Add the onion and cook until softened, about 5 minutes. Add the garlic, reduce heat to low, and cook 1 more minute.

• Add all the remaining ingredients except the salt and red pepper flakes and cook for 5 minutes more, stirring frequently. Transfer the pot to the oven and bake for 20 minutes. Season with salt and red pepper flakes to taste.

Stack the lamb slices and shingle towards the front of the plate.

Finish garnishing the plate with the sauce, eggplant chips and fried basil, if desired.

Main Plates

Some people look at the price of fresh Alaskan salmon and shudder. It is not cheap, for sure, but wild salmon has firmer, less fatty flesh than farm-raised and is worth the cost. We need to look more closely at our food sources to ensure the survival of wild game and natural methods.

Alaskan Salmon Mignon, Poached Hawaiian Hearts of Palm, Yellow Beets and Herb Emulsion

When we speak of the benefits of fish, salmon is at the head of the list. It has great nutritional value, a nice pinkish hue, the healthy kind of fat, and a sweet delicate taste.

This salmon is highlighted in a center-of-the-plate presentation. The hearts of palm are cooked, then placed on the plate and criss-crossed. The salmon, just simply grilled, is placed on top for visual effect and to focus attention on the fish.

Roasted yellow beets are served with a light herb vinaigrette for a flavorful and light accent. Serving the dish in a shallow bowl adds some depth for a great visual effect and makes it easier for your guests to eat.

Alaskan Salmon Mignon, Poached Hawaiian Hearts of Palm, Yellow Beets and Herb Emulsion

Place 2 halves of poached hearts of palm in the center of the bowl. Place 2 more halves on top of the first in the opposite direction.

Place the beet cubes around the plate making a circle surrounding the hearts of palm.

Blanc

1 gallon (16 cups) water

1/2 cup lemon juice

2 onions, finely diced

2 carrots, finely diced

3 ribs celery, finely diced

1/4 cup all-purpose flour

4 sprigs fresh thyme

2 bay leaves

2 tsp salt

• Combine all the ingredients in a large pot and simmer for 8 minutes. Use for cooking hearts of palm, salsify, or artichokes.

Sauce the hearts of palm by lacing the herb emulsion over with a spoon.

Place the salmon on the hearts of palm and garnish with some herbs and two strips of beets.

Main Plates

Consider this dish a blueprint to follow, but feel free to change it as needed. Use shrimp rather then lobster; make a different kind of ravioli; substitute sea bass or snapper. You decide—then go for it.

Trio of Asparagus, Flounder, Beet Ravioli, Poached Lobster and Irish Butter Sauce

A sensible variety of foods on the plate make for a dish that is visually appealing and full of flavor. The key is portion size and using combinations that have natural harmony while at the same time exciting the palate.

This dish uses asparagus as a base for three very simple items that have elegance and style when put together. The presentation lends itself to a straight-line type of styling, and yet it is complemented with natural organic shapes.

Simply seared flounder—the correct word, rather than the often-used but incorrect "sole"—is gently touched with some lemon and pink sea salt and presented with roasted beet ravioli, and then lobster gently poached in butter.

We bring this all together with a classic sauce made with Irish butter—yellow, rich, creamy, and something special.

Contrasting design and flavors are all unified in a dish that is versatile and will linger in the memory.

Trio of Asparagus, Flounder, Beet Ravioli, Poached Lobster and Irish Butter Sauce

Mincing knife

Perfect for cutting small batches of herbs for garnish, this knife features a curved blade that cuts in an easy rocking motion.

Using three poached asparagus halves lay one in the middle facing one side of the plate then place the other two against the one in the middle flowing the opposite direction.

Place the cooked ravioli in the center of the asparagus base.

Irish Butter Sauce

1/3 cup champagne vinegar

1/3 cup dry white wine

Juice from 1/2 lemon

2 shallots, finely chopped

2 sprigs fresh thyme

1/2 cup heavy cream

8 oz unsalted Irish butter, diced and kept cold (regular unsalted butter may be substituted for Irish butter)

Kosher salt to taste

• In a heavy 2-quart saucepan, combine the vinegar, wine, lemon juice, shallots, and thyme. Simmer over medium heat until the mixture is reduced to a wet paste. Add the cream and continue to simmer until reduced to about 2 tablespoons of liquid.

• Reduce the heat to low. Whisk in the chunks of cold butter one or two at a time. Do not let the sauce go over 130°F. or the butter will separate out.

• Season the sauce with salt, strain through a fine-mesh sieve, and serve immediately, or keep covered in a warm place for up to a few hours. Any fresh herb may be added to this sauce for added flavor.

On the either side of the ravioli, place the fish and poached lobster.

Lace the dish with warm butter sauce and fresh minced herbs.

A quality dried pasta from Italy will hold up to a rich and distinctive sauce such as this. Italians use dry pasta as much as fresh, depending on the dish and the sauce. Lasagnette is an ideal pasta for meat sauces and a nice change from spaghetti.

Lasagnette, Ragu of Braised, Crisp and Roasted Veal

Who doesn't enjoy a good pasta? It is, by its very nature, a rustic dish, a dish that is meant to have a flavorful sauce that complements the pasta and gives it interest.

Many chefs have tried to take pasta to new dimensions in order to dazzle people. In many cases, these attempts result in cold pasta or pasta that's lacking essential flavor. Pasta is a great food that does not need to be "played with" too much.

Pasta can be beautifully presented, but that should be achieved by the composition of the sauce. The flavor profiles must all come together for a successful culinary experience. The pasta shown here has layers of flavor and texture—and that "wow factor" that makes the dish come alive.

A bowl with a cover turns this simple dish into an impressive presentation. Try placing a covered bowl in front of a guest and then removing the top. The aroma hits the nose, the eyes come in contact with the food and the experience begins.

Lasagnette, Ragu of Braised, Crisp, and Roasted Veal

To make breading easier, take strips of meat and place in a Ziploc bag, toss in some salt, pepper and flour and shake well. Then place in another bag, add some beaten egg. Remove and repeat with a bag of bread crumbs and fry away.

Take meat from slow-cooked roast and pull into pieces with your hands. Then chop with a knife to the desired size.

Veal Ragu

1/4 cup extra-virgin olive oil

1 onion, finely diced

3 cloves garlic, thinly sliced

3 cups diced veal meat

3 tbsp tomato paste

3/4 cup dry red wine

4 cups canned Italian plum tomatoes

1/4 cup grated Parmigiano-Reggiano

4 fresh basil leaves, minced

1 tsp red pepper flakes

Salt to taste

• Preheat the oven to 300°F. In a large, ovenproof stainless-steel pan, heat the oil. Add the onion and garlic and cook, stirring occasionally, until softened. Add the veal and cook until browned. Add the tomato paste and cook another 2 to 3 minutes. Stir in the red wine and simmer 1 to 2 minutes.

• Add the plum tomatoes, Parmesan, basil, and red pepper flakes, cover the pan and place in the oven. Cook for 90 minutes. Season with salt and serve the ragu over pasta.

Toss cooked pasta with olive oil, salt, sauce, braised meat and roasted meat.

Place pasta in the bowl, top with a cooked artichoke heart and top with some of the meat sauce, then place some of the fried strips of meat around the pasta.

Sear the short ribs the night before. Use a slow cooker or crockpot to cook them all day with a nice broth and veggies. The results are tender and delicious and dinner is no-fuss.

Slow-Cooked Short Rib in Sauce, Roast Mignon of Beef, Garlic Mashed Potatoes and Apple-Glazed Carrots

A nice approach to a protein-rich main course such as beef is to offer smaller portions of the prime cut and then offer a second portion of a braised or slow-roasted cut such as the short rib featured here. The benefits are many: flavors that complement each other, presentations that speak volumes about the food, and a variety of textures.

This plate may seem eccentric, but the concept is sound: a rich protein served in moderation with layers of great flavors. I have always believed that what we eat is not as important as how much of it we eat. The famous Japanese Wagu beef you see on menus here in the States costs about $80 for a steak. That's expensive, particularly because you are paying for a portion that cannot be eaten comfortably. This beef is so rich in fat and flavor that selling or eating an eight-to-ten-ounce steak is insane. In Japan the portion is one to two ounces, dipped in a hot broth or placed on a tableside grill—just the right amount.

Moderation is the key, along with a cool-looking plate that showcases the small portions with the big flavors.

Slow-Cooked Short Rib in Sauce, Roast Mignon of Beef, Garlic Mashed Potatoes and Apple-Glazed Carrots

Food Mill

A kitchen essential that quickly and easily mashes and purées—perfect for homemade tomato sauce and creamy mashed potatoes.

To make a great mashed potato, use a ricer to puree the potatoes as shown. Rice them twice then fold in butter, some hot cream and see the velvety results.

Make a quenelle with the potatoes by taking two spoons, fill one spoon then shape and turn with the other spoon. Do this one to two times for a simple but eye-appealing effect.

Apple Glaze for Root Vegetables

2 Granny Smith apples, peeled, cored, and roughly chopped

1 cup apple-cider vinegar

1 cup apple cider

1/4 cup granulated sugar

1 tbsp minced shallot

4 sprigs fresh thyme

1 sprig fresh sage

Salt and freshly ground black pepper to taste

• In a small saucepan, combine the apples, vinegar, cider, sugar, shallot, thyme and sage and bring to a boil over medium-high heat. Reduce the heat to medium-low and simmer until the apples are translucent and soft and the vinegar has reduced by half, about 15 minutes. Remove from the heat and cool for at least 10 minutes. Remove and discard the herb sprigs.

• Once cool, transfer to a blender or food processor and puree until smooth. Taste the glaze and season with salt and pepper.

Take the cooked filet mignon and slice evenly. This makes the presentation look elegant and helps you control the portion.

Glaze the carrots with some meat juices from the cooking, Place all components on the plate, sauce the short ribs, spike the mashed potatoes with some extra-virgin olive oil, and place sea salt on the meat right before service. Salting prior drains the meat of its natural juices.

Family style is a great way to serve food to guests. Present the meal on attractive platters or large plates for people to pass around. It's convenient, simple, and allows guests to take as much or as little as they would like.

Culinary Flair for Family Style

"Buy it or make it yourself, but serve it in style for your guests in a simple but elegant manner that will have them asking for seconds."

In today's rushed world of work and family, purchasing pre-made and pre-cooked foods is no longer an occasional thing. For many, it's a way of life. Even in the professional kitchen chefs may buy "pre-scratch" foods, already prepared foods, and even fresh foods that are ready to cook. There are many reasons for this: busy kitchens, small labor budgets, little kitchen space and large volume.

One advantage to purchasing already prepared food or even complete dinners is that you can enjoy your meal at home and still have family time or time to spend with your guests. In many of my kitchens, we sell already cooked meals for holidays or special occasions. During my restaurant years, we often got requests for complete meals to go and we always happily complied.

This section will show you that even if you did buy the roasted chicken, the potato salad, the dim sum, or the sushi, you can add special touches to the plate to make it look like your own. Many other items in the book can be purchased half cooked or pre-cooked and then brought to the table with your signature look.

As we show you here, just because the food was purchased or served family-style does not mean you cannot serve it with the same culinary flair as single plates.

Even your sides can be dressed up. Add culinary flair by serving hot mashed potatoes with a dab of butter melting in the dish, some chopped herbs over the vegetables and add a lacing of extra-virgin olive oil.

Is It Mom's Roast Chicken Dinner?

Roasted or rotisserie chicken is a great grab-and-go item available from almost any supermarket or upscale food store and from many ethnic markets and fast-food outlets as well. Buy a few simple vegetables to accompany it, or even some pre-made sides, and you have a great family dinner.

Buying the chicken already cooked saves effort and clean-up in the kitchen and gives you more quality time to spend with your family at night or on the weekend. Convenience food, however, does not need to look convenient when served at the table. Pre-carving and trimming the chicken will go a long way toward creating the classic "home cooked" ambiance. Add gravy, seasoned vegetables and some other sides, and you have a dinner to be proud of. We present this classic on a large plate. A few quick strokes of the knife make the chicken look even more impressive.

Take a few minutes to do some simple things like heating the gravy in a pan then whisking in some cold butter and a few sprigs of thyme. Sauté the vegetables in a pan with your favorite oil or butter, then add some of your own flavor bites. Creating culinary flair is always worth a few minutes of your time.

Is It Mom's Roast Chicken Dinner?

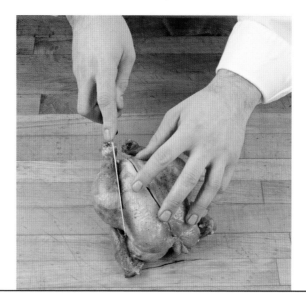

Using a knife, carefully remove the breast meat from the chicken. Then carefully remove the leg and thigh meat.

Slice the breast on a slight angle. Using a spatula, pick up the sliced breast meat and place back onto the chicken carcass.

Paring Knife

A small utility knife is especially useful for peeling and shaping fruits, vegetables and even meats. The short blade and firm handles give you plenty of control.

Chicken Pan Gravy

Pan gravy is a classic American sauce that uses the natural juices and fats left over in the pan after roasting chicken, chops, steaks, etc.

• For each cup of gravy you would like, combine 2 tablespoons of pan juices and 2 tablespoons flour in a small pan and cook over low heat, stirring, until the mixture is bubbling and brown. Stir 1 cup of the liquid from the roasting pan (or stock) into the mixture and whisk briskly. Then whisk in 2 to 3 tablespoons of the fat from the pan and season the gravy with salt and pepper to taste.

• For a richer gravy, whisk in 1/4 cup of heavy cream along with the liquid.

• Remember that when roasting a chicken or roast, make sure you have some broth in the pan and continually baste; do not let the pan dry out—add a little broth, water or butter.

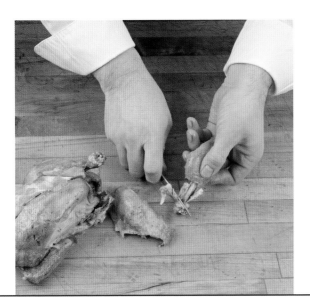

Separate the leg and thigh with a knife. Using a small sharp knife, scrape the end of the leg bone to expose the end of the bone.

Place chicken onto a large serving dish. Place vegetables next to the chicken. Place potatoes in a separate bowl and serve with the chicken. Finish the chicken with gravy and serve immediately.

First cover the inside of the mold with a touch of olive oil, then arrange the tomatoes. Pack the salad firmly and let sit for a hour. You can even layer the salads for a more dramatic effect and better flavor profile.

Couscous Salad

I am not a big fan of cold pasta salads with carelessly chopped, uncooked vegetables covered in mayonnaise. In Italy, there is no such dish—hot pasta is tossed with fresh garden vegetables and finished with a light dressing or simply good olive oil.

I know, however, that there is a need for such salads for buffets, cookouts and the like, so I'll compromise a bit. For me, that means giving the mundane the culinary flair it deserves.

Our version uses Israeli couscous made from semolina wheat. It is available in small pearl and large pearl versions. Good couscous takes time to cook and is usually steamed. You can, however, purchase partially cooked and fully cooked versions in stores. It is a nice item to use as a salad.

Instead of just mixing the salad and tossing it in a bowl, a simple but effective technique can give this or any salad some flair. A cake ring, nicely sliced tomatoes, seasonal vegetables and a garnish of greens and dried tomatoes make this salad stand out.

Any dressing can be used for this type of presentation. Creamy dressings hold together better than lighter dressings. You can also use this technique for lentils, bulgur wheat and other grains. At the end of the day, it's up to you.

Couscous Salad

Place large ring mold on a serving plate and line with thin slices of Roma tomatoes.

Fill inside of mold with couscous salad. Even out top of salad by gently pressing down with tamper or back of large spoon.

Couscous Salad

1/4 cup lemon juice

2 tsp Dijon mustard

1/2 tsp kosher salt

1 cup extra-virgin olive oil

1 lb couscous, cooked and cooled slightly

6 scallions, trimmed and thinly sliced

4 tomatoes, peeled, seeded, and diced

1 green bell pepper, seeds and membranes removed, diced

1/2 cup chopped parsley

1/3 cup chopped dill

• Combine lemon juice, mustard, and salt in a small bowl. Slowly whisk in the olive oil.

• In a large bowl, toss together the couscous, scallions, tomatoes, bell pepper, parsley, and dill. Drizzle with the dressing and toss again. Refrigerate for at least 1 hour or overnight.

Place a small pile of dressed mixed greens on top of the salad.

Remove metal ring mold, arrange tomato crisps around mixed greens and serve.

With this method of garnishing and its sure-fire impact, use your creativity to think of unique ways to present all of your salads. No longer do salads need to be placed in bowls. Think of adding additional flavor by marinating the vegetable slices or fruits prior to lining your mold.

Potato Salad, Torte-Style

Potato salad is a staple of family barbeques, picnics, and outdoor grilling. There are many variations on potato salad. German-style is made with warm sweet and sour vinaigrette with lardons of bacon. The elegant potato salad from France is finished with house-made dressing and sometimes laced with truffle and egg. This may sound like overkill, but the marriage of potatoes, egg, and truffle makes for a simple yet delicious union.

Some prefer a simple combination of perfectly cooked potatoes, mayonnaise, celery, boiled eggs, and salt and pepper. Potato salad, as with many foods, can be purchased as well. Even if you buy a quart of potato salad at your favorite deli, with just a few easy steps you can present a dish that will ensure "wows" at the table. No one will even suspect it was purchased.

Even with a bought product, you can enhance the flavor with a drizzle of quality olive oil, some chopped eggs, a spoon or two of your favorite dressing or mayonnaise, and spices. Whatever your fancy, our simple but stunning presentation is easily done using a ring or cake mold from the pastry shop.

Potato Salad
Torte Style

Place large ring mold on a large serving plate. Line mold with thin strips of zucchini.

Fill the center of ring mold with potato salad. Press salad gently into the mold with the back of a spoon until it is spread evenly.

Ring

Rings come in a variety of sizes and may be seamless or riveted together, creating a minor crease in the mold. They typically range in size from 2 inches to 12 inches in diameter and 1 to 4 inches high.

Potato Salad Dressing

2 cups mayonnaise

1/4 cup Dijon mustard

1/4 cup finely chopped
  dill pickles

1/4 cup dill pickle juice

2 tbsp drained capers

2 tbsp chopped fresh
  flat-leaf parsley

1/2 bunch dill, chopped

1/2 lemon, juiced

• In a large stainless-steel mixing bowl, whisk together all the ingredients. This dressing can made ahead of time and kept in the refrigerator. Just add cooked potatoes, hard-cooked eggs, scallions, red onion, and salt and pepper to taste for a delightful salad.

Arrange hard cooked egg quarters around outside of the salad to form a ring around the top. Fill center of eggs with marinated celery.

Place a pancetta crisp on top of salad. When ready to serve, remove the ring mold.

When handling wasabi or ginger, always wash your hands completely to ensure you do not get a surprise when your fingers touch your mouth.

Sushi At Home

The sushi craze is still going strong. You can buy sushi at restaurants, grocery stores, and even airports. Sushi, which means "seasoned rice", is often confused with sashimi, which is sliced raw fish. They are two different items. What vegetarian sushi, dessert sushi, and other non-traditional versions of sushi have in common is the tangy, vinegar-seasoned rice used as the foundation.

Purchasing quality sushi is easy, and taking the time to present the sushi attractively at home is indeed worth the effort. The best thing about buying food already prepared from a restaurant or market is the convenience and saving of valuable time. Then taking the small amount of time to present the food in a simple but elegant manner gives dinner the "home touch" that epitomizes what the family meal should be. There is nothing worse, in my view, than eating Chinese food or sushi out of the cardboard and plastic containers they come in.

Here we take basic purchased sushi and use a stylish plate that will offer some visual impact. We then take the ginger and the wasabi and with a few tricks transform the store bought sushi into a stunning presentation—what I call "eye candy." So, take those of couple extra minutes to show off the food to best effect and demonstrate to the diners that they are important, especially if they are your family.

148

Take a slice of pickled ginger and roll to form center of flower. Continue to wrap slices of pickled ginger to complete the flower shape.

Place the pickled ginger rose in lower center section of plate. Fill a small cup with soy sauce and place in the upper center portion of plate.

Sushi Dipping Sauce

1/2 cup mirin or sake

1/2 cup dark soy sauce

1 tsp granulated sugar

1 tsp grated fresh ginger

• In a small saucepan over medium-low heat, combine the mirin, soy sauce, and sugar. Cook until the sugar dissolves. Transfer to a bowl, add ginger, and allow to cool before serving.

Using two small spoons, form two quenelles of
wasabi paste and place one to either side of soy sauce.

Arrange pieces of sushi in other sections of plate.
Create visual effect by alternating colors and
types of sushi.

When using purchased puff pastry, defrost a sheet from the freezer in your refrigerator. Lightly roll out with a rolling pin for best results. Make your tartin then place it in the refrigerator for 15 minutes. Puff pastry cooks best when cold.

1-2-3 Tomato Tartin

Okay, perhaps you can't purchase an already-made tomato tartin, but that should not deny you the pleasure of this simple but flavorful dish.

Purchase the puff pastry already made, if you are not up to peeling and seeding fresh tomatoes, purchase quality Italian whole tomatoes in a can. Team that with fresh basil leaves, extra virgin olive oil, and grated Parmigiano Reggiano cheese and you are on the way.

You might be asking, "What is the presentation? What big-time chef's trick is involved here?" Well, it is all in the dish itself. There are times when good food says what is has to say without a lot of tricks of the trade.

The presentation is in the cooking of the puff pastry to a rich golden brown and in the green of the basil against the red of the simmered tomatoes laced with olive oil, all topped with grated cheese of the finest quality.

If you truly eat with your eyes, this tartin will have you hungry in no time. When serving, place the tartin on the plate and add just a touch of fine aged balsamic to complete the experience.

Culinary flair in its simplest form is what this pleasing dish is about.

1-2-3 Tomato Tartin

Pizza Cutter

A pizza cutter can be found in almost every kitchen, but keep it sharp to ensure a straight cut without disturbing your favorite toppings.

Remove tomato tartin from pan and place on cutting board. Using a pizza cutter or sharp knife, cut tartin into desired portion size.

Place tartin pieces onto serving plate. Lightly drizzle olive oil over tartin. Place fresh basil and grated cheese on the tartin.

Olive Oil Tomatoes

4 plum tomatoes, peeled, seeded, and quartered

2 cloves garlic, thinly sliced

1/2 cup olive oil, plus more as needed

1 tsp sugar

2 tsp kosher salt

1 tsp crushed red pepper flakes

• Place tomato quarters in a bowl with garlic, 1/2 cup of olive oil, sugar, salt, and red pepper and toss gently. Spread evenly in a small baking pan, adding more oil to ensure the tomatoes are covered with oil. Place in a 175°F. oven for 1 hour

• Carefully remove the tomatoes from the oil. Refrigerate tomatoes and oil separately.

For service, place a piece of the tartin on a small
service plate and add balsamic syrup to finish of
the plate.

Using a Chinese bamboo steam basket at home is easy to do. You can keep dim sum in your freezer, always ready for guests or family. When cooking them, always line the basket with bok choy leaves to prevent the dim sum from sticking.

Yum Yum Dim Sum

Everyone loves small bites of food. In Chinese cooking small bites are a tradition. The Chinese tea snacks called "dim sum", which literally means "to touch the heart", consist of a variety of dumplings, steamed dishes, and other small-bite goodies. Similar in concept to hors d'oeuvres, appetizers, or amuse bouche, dim sum is awesome.

I remember my first visit to a dim sum restaurant with chef and TV personality Martin Yan. We ate and sampled all of the delicacies from the passing dim sum carts. The highlight of the meal was when the chef arranged for us to visit the kitchen and see how these great little bites were made by hand.

These items can be purchased in many ways: from the frozen food section of fine markets or Asian food stores, by ordering dim sum to go at your favorite Chinese restaurant, or by buying them fresh and cooking them at home.

Given the simplicity of dim sum, the presentation of these small bites should be simple and clean, focusing on the food with no gimmicks.

We steam Chinese cabbage or bok choy leaves to line a large plate and provide a showcase for the dim sum. Some dried lemon slices and a glaze of sauce along with flavor bites of sesame seed and finely cut spring onion keep the integrity of the cuisine while enhancing the look of the food.

Yum Yum Dim Sum

Lay a blanched leaf of bok choy on the serving plate. It may be necessary to use more than one piece to cover the plate.

Fill a small cup with dipping sauce and place towards the top of the plate.

Dried Myer Lemons

1 cup granulated sugar

1 cup water

1 sprig fresh thyme

2 Meyer lemons

- Place the sugar, water, and thyme in a stainless-steel saucepan. Place over medium heat and bring to a boil. Remove from the heat and set aside.

- Meanwhile, with a sharp knife or mandoline, slice the lemons into 1/8-inch-thick slices. Place the slices in the hot sugar solution and allow to steep for 5 minutes. Remove the slices with a slotted spoon and lay them on a sheet pan covered with a silicone baking mat.

- Place the sheet pan in a 200°F. oven and dry the slices until crisp, about 1 hour.

- Once the slices are dried and crisp, transfer them to an airtight container until needed. The remaining syrup may be reserved and reused.

Place different types of dim sum on top of the bok choy in straight lines starting near the dipping sauce.

Sprinkle toasted sesame seeds and minced chives over dim sum. Finish plate with dried lemons and serve.

Family Style

Dessert is the grand finale, the end to a perfect evening or a perfect day, and everyone who enjoys food loves a great sweet treat.

Subtle Structure with Dessert

"The show stealer, the course you save room for, the course for indulgence."

Tempting the sweet tooth is an easy task. Most people have their favorite dessert—chocolate, ice cream, pies, rich layer cakes—something the person just cannot resist. One the most famous lines when a meal is left unfinished is, "I'm saving room for dessert."

The presentation of pastry through the years has evolved into complex shapes and architectural designs that almost dare you to eat them. But, sometimes the component of flavor is lost and the impact of simplicity completely forgotten.

In sweet courses, as in savory, no matter how good food may look it primarily needs to taste good. It should make the taste buds come alive and desire more. Presentation and taste go hand in hand. We have featured simple preparations, but this is my way of showing that any dessert can be plated with a pleasing, subtle structure that emphasizes the "wow" factor. The desserts featured here are favorites of dessert lovers everywhere: chocolate cream pie, cheesecake, ice cream, cookies and a crumble.

Even timeless desserts that withstand changes and fads still need the red carpet treatment when presented at the table. All of our desserts are presented on plates with shapes other than round to show that something as subtle as the china can make a difference.

Go ahead, dive in and indulge. I know you saved room for dessert!

Try using two or three different kinds of apples for a contrast of
tart and sweet flavors.

Baked Apple Cobbler, Mascarpone Ice Cream and a Caramel Disk

Desserts designed by today's pastry chefs have a whole new direction with herbs, salt and spices complementing chocolate and other sweet flavors. However, there is nothing like the memory of comfort desserts: deep-dish pies, rich layer cakes and cookies fresh out of the oven.

Apple crumble, cobblers and baked apple crisp are old-time favorites. Our crumble features apple pieces slowly baked with raisins, butter, brown sugar and spices.

We then finish it off with a crumble topping of nuts, flour and brown sugar. The contrast between hot and cold has always been special. The warmth of a crisp dough or pastry topped by a cold, creamy rich ice cream tantalizes the taste buds.

The structure and presentation is subtle but effective with the caramel disk giving the dish a nice look and a bit of a candy touch.

Baked Apple Cobbler, Mascarpone Ice Cream and Caramel Disk

Silpat

Modern flexible, silicone-coated fiberglass mats with a clean, non-stick surface for baking.

Spoon some of the warm caramelized sugar onto the Silpat while moving in a circular motion to create spiral effect. Allow the sugar to cool completely before handling.

Using a small spatula, gently remove the sugar disks from the Silpat.

Crumble Topping

3/4 cup cake flour

3/4 cup brown sugar

3/4 cup old-fashioned
 rolled oats

1/3 cup chopped
 toasted pecans

2 tsp maple syrup

1/2 tsp vanilla powder

1/2 tsp ground cinnamon

Pinch ground cloves

1/4 tsp kosher salt

1/2 cup high-quality
 butter, cut into pieces

• Combine the flour, brown sugar, oats, pecans, maple syrup, vanilla, cinnamon, cloves, and salt in a large bowl and stir until well mixed. With a pastry blender or two knives, cut the butter into the flour and oat mixture until crumbled and no pieces of butter larger than peas remain.

Place the baked cobbler on a serving plate.
Place a small scoop of the ice cream in the center
of the cobbler.

Place the caramel sugar decoration on the ice cream
for a simple but dramatic look. These garnishes
can be made ahead of time and kept in an
airtight container.

Use fruit combinations that you enjoy and flavors that harmonize well. For example, the blueberries featured would go well with a dollop of lemon curd rather than the sauce shown.

Cheesecake, Blueberry Compote, Candied Orange and Chocolate Stick

Cheesecake has stood the test of time, and one stop at a Cheesecake Factory restaurant reveals the wide variety of flavors and varieties available.

Cheesecake can be made with different cheeses that can lighten the texture of the cake or even give it a slightly tart flavor. The crust can be enhanced by using Oreo cookies, vanilla wafers, chocolate graham crackers and so forth.

As you see here, a slice of cheesecake becomes more than just a slice of cheesecake with some simple garnish. From the berries, the coulis, the candied orange, the chocolate dipped cookie and the layout of the items—this cheesecake speaks a whole new language. The few extra minutes it takes to do this will have your guest looking at this familiar dessert in a whole new way.

Cheesecake, Blueberry Compote, Candied Orange and Chocolate Stick

Pastry Tip

This simple tool attached to the end of a pastry bag or in the corner of a plastic bag will make your whipped topping look professional.

Take some honey or simple syrup and with a small paintbrush make six dots on the plate in a line on a slight angle. Place a berry on each dot. This will cause the berries to stick to the plate and give a hint of sweetness.

Place the slice of cheesecake on a slight angle from the berries for contrast.

Blueberry Compote

1/2 cup blueberry juice or other berry juice

3 tbsp raw sugar

2 tsp arrowroot or cornstarch

Pinch vanilla powder

2 cups fresh or frozen wild Maine blueberries (no sugar added)

• Place all the ingredients except the blueberries in a small saucepan and stir to combine. Cook over medium heat, stirring constantly, until clear and slightly thickened.

• Add the blueberries and cook until heated through. Divide into 2 servings.

Garnish the top of the cheesecake with cream and berries.

Place the chocolate stick. And then make a nice puddle of raspberry coulis away from the point of the cake.

The warm cookie finished with a strip of peanuts is effective and keeps the integrity of a dessert that needs no dramatic garnish for the guest to enjoy.

Chocolate Peanut Butter Pie,
Warm Cookie and Spiced Peanuts

Desserts, as with savory dishes, should exhibit the harmony of great flavor combinations that spell success for a dish.

Lemon and blueberry, strawberry and basil, apple and cinnamon and chocolate and peanut butter are perfect examples.

Chocolate and peanut butter are indeed a natural. The endless variety of cookies, cakes and processed offerings available using this combination proves that it goes a long way in stirring up excitement.

I have even designed a handmade peanut butter cup that would give a certain brand a run for its money!

Our peanut butter pie features a peanut crust, a layer of smooth peanut butter mousse and a generous chocolate cream filling. The topping of fresh whipped cream and quality chocolate shavings makes it even more tempting.

Chocolate Peanut Butter Pie, Warm Cookie and Spiced Peanuts

Using a small paintbrush, brush a line of creamy peanut butter or honey across the plate in a straight line on an angle from the plate design.

Take some roasted, chopped peanuts and place on the honey.

Spiced Peanuts

1/4 cup kosher salt

3 tablespoons
 granulated sugar

1 tsp vanilla powder

2 tsp cocoa powder

1 tsp curry powder

1 1/2 tsp ground cinnamon

1 1/2 tsp ground cumin

1/2 tsp cayenne pepper

1 tbsp roasted peanut oil

1 lb unsalted dry-roasted
 peanuts, preferably
 organic or all-natural
 unprocessed

• Combine the salt, sugar, vanilla, and cocoa in a medium bowl.

• In a small nonstick sauté pan over low heat, combine the curry, cinnamon, cumin, and cayenne and toast, shaking the pan, until very fragrant, 2 to 3 minutes; this brings out the oils and flavors of the spices.

• Transfer the spices to the bowl with sugar and mix well; cover and let sit for 2 hours.

• In the pan that the spices cooked in, heat the oil over medium heat. Add the peanuts and cook, stirring, 2 to 3 minutes. Transfer the nuts to a large bowl. Sprinkle them with 2 to 3 tablespoons of the spice mix and toss until coated.

With a grater or a peeler shave chocolate curls on top of the tart before plating.

Place the cookie and tart on the plate. A touch of melted chocolate or peanut butter on the bottom of the tart and cookie will prevent them from sliding and add a flavor bite.

If you do not want to make a traditional custard, buy a prepared version or go to your favorite pastry shop and ask if you can purchase a quart of pastry cream or vanilla bean pudding.

De-Constructed English Trifle

During my time working and training in England, one of my favorite puddings ("desserts" in the USA) was trifle. From the top, this classic dessert looks like a bowl full of whipped cream, but through the side of its traditional glass serving bowl, you can see layers of pudding, cake and fruit. The flavors of sherry, custard cream, candied fruits, cake, and jam blend together like a sweet casserole. Quite simply, it is pure pleasure.

Our version is a bit lighter and offers a presentation that we call "de-constructed", showcasing the ingredients in their purest form.

A rich custard made with brandy is layered between rows of fresh berries, sponge cake soaked with raspberry coulis, and jam and then topped with some candied orange.

If you want to go all the way, add dollops of fresh whipped cream and sprinkle with almonds and for a moment you may think you are in an English home enjoying High Tea.

De-Constructed English Trifle

Spoon or pipe the pastry cream across the plate in two rows spaced about one third from each end.

In the middle, between the two rows of pastry cream, place cubed pieces of pound cake or sponge cake.

Vanilla Pudding

3/4 cup organic
    white sugar

2 tbsp cornstarch

1 tbsp arrowroot

1/4 tsp kosher salt

1 cup milk

1 cup light cream

2 vanilla beans, split

2 lightly beaten egg yolks

2 tbsp diced cold
    unsalted butter

• In a small bowl, whisk together 1/2 cup of the sugar, the cornstarch, arrowroot, and salt. Pour the milk and cream into a stainless-steel saucepan and whisk in the sugar mixture. Add the vanilla beans and place over medium heat. Cook, stirring constantly with a wooden spoon, until thickened and bubbly. Lower the heat if necessary to avoid burning the mixture and cook, still stirring, 2 more minutes. Remove from the heat. Remove and discard the vanilla beans.

• In a large bowl, whisk together the egg yolks and remaining 1/4 cup sugar. Whisk a small amount of hot milk mixture into yolks, then slowly whisk the yolk mixture back into the saucepan. Cook, stirring, 2 more minutes.

• Remove from the heat; whisk in the butter and immediately pour into a bowl. Cover and refrigerate.

Place berries to the left and right side of the pastry cream.

Drizzle the cake with raspberry coulis and then top the pudding with some candied orange pieces.

The ice cream sandwiches can be made as much as five days ahead, just wrap individually and tightly and take out at least 3-5 minutes before serving to temper the ice cream and the cookies.

Home-Made Ice Cream Sandwich with Banana Sheets

Ice cream and chocolate chip cookies are natural teammates. There are two choices with this dessert. You can buy a commercial version full of chemicals and corn syrup, or take the time to make, bake, or buy the components for a simple but elegant dessert that will get you accolades.

All it takes is your favorite jumbo or small chewy cookie, freshly made or quality bought ice cream, a few garnishes, and you are on the way.

We serve this dessert on a rectangular plate with the sandwich in an upright position. The cookie straw and shaved banana make for a subtle but effective presentation. You might want to serve it with a fork or spoon, but hands will quickly take over.

If you seek more indulgence, add some chocolate ganache or hot fudge to dip the sandwich in.

Home-Made Ice Cream Sandwich with Banana Sheets

To make the sandwich, scoop the ice cream and place between 2 sheets of plastic wrap, then press to form a disk. Place in freezer while prepping cookies.

Spread some chocolate ganache on the cookies and place the ice cream disk between two cookies to make your sandwich.

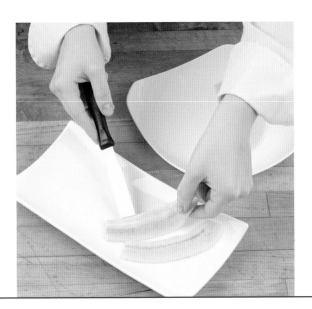

Shave a firm banana on the mandolin to make your sheets and place them on the plate.

Spoon a dollop of warm ganache off to one side of the plate opposite the banana slices. Place the ice cream sandwich on end in the ganache. Finish plate by leaning a pirouette onto the sandwich.

The base of ice cream is a custard sauce, and with today's home machines, making your own has never been easier. Try it and taste the difference, especially with the fresh fruit and quality of flavor bites you can add.

Trio of Ice Creams with Independent Garnish

Ice cream is an all-time favorite, and quality ice cream is one of those desserts that tell us, "Do not mess with me too much. I am sufficiently good and special as I am." We need, however, to create a little love here, a little something special with a bit of structure and the "wow" factor.

I can't take a lot of credit on this one; the plate does it all. The three wells let you serve three flavors, or perhaps just one. Whatever you desire. The key is to top each ice cream with a garnish that is flavorful but not tacky like those commercial ice cream sauces. Use quality ingredients: real strawberry puree, rich chocolate sauce, real vanilla bean syrup. Texture is also important. Cookie crumbs the same flavor as the ice cream base or chocolate decorations both give height and extra flavor. Go on - indulge yourself!

Trio of Ice Creams with Independent Garnish

Place a cookie in the center of each plate well.

Place 1 scoop of each flavored ice cream onto the cookie bases.

Making Ganache

- To make a glaze or coating: 1 part heavy cream to 3 parts chocolate; use 2 tablespoons cocoa butter and 1 tablespoon butter for every cup of cream.

- To make a truffle filling: 1 part heavy cream to 2 parts chocolate; use 4 tablespoons cocoa butter for every cup of cream.

- To make a light filling: 1 part heavy cream to 1 part chocolate; use 1 tablespoon cocoa butter for every cup of cream.

- General directions: Bring cream and butter just to a boil. Pour the hot cream over chopped chocolate; let it sit a minute or two and then whisk until smooth.

Ganache is widely used in the pastry kitchen. When barely warm and liquid, it can be poured over a cake or torte to make a smooth, shiny glaze. If cooled to room temperature, it becomes a spreadable filling and frosting. Refrigerated, ganache can be whipped and then used as a filling or frosting, or formed into truffles.

The taste and quality of ganache is primarily dependent on the quality of the cream and, most especially, the chocolate you start with—not all chocolates are the same.

Garnish each ice cream with sauce that reflects the flavor of the ice cream.

On top of each scoop place a garnish such as glazed whole fruit, chocolate decorations, cookie or cake crumbles.

Resources for the Kitchen

Fortessa Professional quality tableware for the home, including the plates used throughout this book. www.fortessa.com

Kitchen Aid For great culinary items and professional kitchen type equipment. Kitchenaid.com

Chefs Warehouse An incredible source of food products for the professional chef available for the home cook as well. www.allthingsculinarygroup.com

The Cook's Warehouse An excellent supplier of tools and equipment for the professional chef and the home cook. www.cookswarehouse.com

GigaChef An educational website devoted to chefs, culinarians and foodies. www.gigachef.com

Crate & Barrel A store of uncompromising quality for housewares, china, tools for cooks and furniture. The Fortessa Cuisine Collection dinnerware featured in this book can be purchased at Crate & Barrel. www.CrateandBarrel.com

JB Prince A store in New York that has awesome tools and books. You can cook with tools that the professional chef uses everyday in their kitchens. www.jbprince.com

American Culinary Federation (ACF) The largest professional chefs federation now with a membership for Culinary Enthusiast, for anyone with a passion for the culinary arts. Home cooks and gourmets are welcome. www.acfchefs.org

Chef Leonard's Suggested Culinary Books

The Perfectionist: Life and Death in Haute Cuisine, Rudolph Chelminshi

The Devil in the Kitchen: the Making of a Great Chef, Marco Pierre White

In Search of Perfection: Reinventing Kitchen Classics, Heston Blumenthal

Martin Yan's Feast: The Best of Yan Can Cook, Martin Yan, Jacques Pepin

The Way To Cook, Julia Child

Tasting Club, Dina Cheney

Mastering Simplicity, A Life in the Kitchen, Christian Delouvrier

The Cooking of Italy, Foods of The World Series Time Life 1968 Original version; Waverly Root

Essentials of Classic Italian Cooking, Marcella Hazan, Karin Kretschmann

Great American Food, Charlie Palmer

Tastes and Tales of a Chef; The Apprentice's Journey, Edward Leonard

Club Cuisine: Cooking with a Master Chef, Edward G. Leonard

Common Cooking Measurement Equivalents

1/16 teaspoon	dash
1/8 teaspoon	a pinch
1 tablespoon (tbsp)	3 teaspoons (tsp)
1/16 cup (c)	1 tablespoon
1/8 cup	2 tablespoons
1/6 cup	2 tablespoons + 2 teaspoons
1/4 cup	4 tablespoons
1/3 cup	5 tablespoons + 1 teaspoon
3/8 cup	6 tablespoons
1/2 cup	8 tablespoons
2/3 cup	10 tablespoons + 2 teaspoons
3/4 cup	12 tablespoons
1 cup	48 teaspoons
1 cup	16 tablespoons
8 fluid ounces (fl oz)	1 cup
1 pint (pt)	2 cups
1 quart (qt)	2 pints
4 cups	1 quart
1 gallon (gal)	4 quarts
16 ounces (oz)	1 pound (lb)

Glossary

Accouterments: Items that go with the main dish, a fancy word for side plates, sauces, syrups, etc.

Acidulated Water: Water with lemon juice or other acid added, intended to keep raw fruit or vegetables from discoloring.

Adobo Sauce: Seasoning paste used in Mexican cuisine made with ground chiles, herbs and vinegar.

Albumin: Clarifying protein found in egg whites, leeks, blood, and connective tissue.
  • Soluble in cold liquid.
  • It congeals when heated and traps impurities.

Al Dente: Cooked to the point of tenderness but with some texture remaining.

A la Minute: At the last minute, just before service.

Au Jus: Served with unthickened pan juices, often with the addition of stock or other flavorings.

Bain-Marie: A hot water bath used to insure gentle cooking. Water is placed in a pan and other foods, in separate containers, are set into the water; the whole is then usually placed in the oven. Also, a double boiler insert for slow cooking over simmering water. Also, a steam table in which smaller pans and their contents are kept hot.

Barding: Wrapping meats with thin slices of fat or fatty meats, like bacon, before cooking.

Bechamel: Basic white sauce.

Beurre Manié: A 60/40 mix of whole butter and flour used as a liaison.

Bird Chiles: Slender, straight, chiles, bitingly hot and resembling the arbol.

Blanch: To immerse food briefly in boiling water, either to help loosen the skin or to precook briefly to set color and flavor.

Boil: To cook liquid rapidly so that bubbles constantly rise and break on the surface. To cook food in boiling liquid.

Bouquet Garni: Little bundles of herbs and spices, usually wrapped in cheesecloth.
- Classic combination – parsley, peppercorns, thyme, and bay leaves.

Braise: To cook a seared product in a tightly covered pan with varying amounts of a flavorful liquid for a lengthy period of time.
- Best for tough cuts of meat.
- Usually completed in the oven.
- Braised vegetables are usually not seared.

Bread: To coat with bread or cracker crumbs before cooking, usually after first dipping food into beaten egg or other liquid so crumbs will adhere.

Brine: A salt solution. Also the act of soaking a product in a salt solution.

Brown: To cook in a small amount of fat until browned on all sides, giving food an appetizing color and flavor and, in meats, sealing in natural juices.

Brunoise: To dice vegetable minutely, or the resulting diced vegetable mixture.

Capon: Castrated and fattened rooster.

Carryover Cooking: The cooking that takes place after a product is removed from the oven.
- Remove roasts from the oven at least 5 degrees below the desired temperature.

Chard: A member of the beet family that produces large leaves and thick stalks.

Chèvre: Goat's milk cheese.

Chiffonade: To finely cut greens to produce thin strips.

Chinois: A metal, conical strainer with fine-mesh. Sometimes known as a "China cap."

Concasser: To chop roughly – often used to describe a rough chop of blanched, peeled, and seeded tomatoes.

Confit: Meats cooked and preserved in fat. Fruits preserved in sugar or liquor.

Consommé: Clarified stock that has been fortified with lean ground meat and additional mirepoix and bouquet garni.

- **Contrast:** The difference in color, texture and shapes used in the preparation of food

Coral: The roe of lobster or other crustaceans.

Court-Bouillon: A poaching liquid that contains water, an acid (wine, citrus, vinegar), aromatics and other flavorings.
- Acids help flavor and coagulate the proteins of the products being poached.

Cube: To cut into small cubes (about 1/2 inch). In meats, to tenderize by pounding with a special tool that imprints a checkered pattern on the surface, breaking tough fibers to increase tenderness.

Culinary template: A pre-developed plan or layout used to create a dish or plating style from a design, pattern, type of plating or style

Darne: A thick slice of a large raw fish.

Dash: A very small amount, less than 1/8 teaspoon.

Deglaze: To dissolve and pick up the flavorful bits left on the bottom of a pan after cooking.
- Acids like wine work best because they help extract flavor.
- Stock, water or other liquids can also be used.

Demi-glace: "Half glaze" — a brown sauce reduction.

Depouillage: To skim the impurities off the top of a stock, soup or sauce.

Dice: To cut into very small pieces.
(about 1/8 to 1/4 inch)

Dredge: To coat or cover food lightly but completely with flour, sugar, or other fine substance.

Emulsion: A mixture of one liquid with another with which it cannot normally combine smoothly.

EVOO: Extra Virgin Olive Oil

Farce: Stuffing or forcemeat.

Fat: Generic term for butter, margarine, lard or vegetable shortening; also the rendered drippings of meat or fowl.

Fat Cap: Layer of fat that surrounds muscle tissue.

Fines Herbes: A fine mixture of fresh herbs used to season meats, fish and sauces.

Flavor Bites: Added spices, herbs, salts, flavored butters and oils. Items that enhance the flavor of a dish.

Flavor Profiles: The flavors that make up a dish, example: a apple pie's flavor profile would be the tartness of the apple, sugar, cinnamon, cloves, allspice, butter and the pastry.

Foie Gras: Fattened goose or duck liver.

Foundation foods: The foods that the dishes are built on.

Fry: To cook in hot fat — pan-frying in a skillet (very little fat) or deep-frying in a heavy pan (food immersed in fat).

Fumet: White stock with other flavorings added, simmered and reduced by 50%.

Galanga: A root that is a relative of ginger, used in Thai cuisine — sometimes spelled galangal.

Glacé: Brown stock reduced by 85% to 90%.

Grease: To rub fat or oil on a cooking surface or utensil to prevent food from sticking.

Grill: To cook on a rack over direct heat - gas, electricity, or charcoal; to broil on a grill.

Haricot Vert: Thin French green beans.

Herbs: Leaves of plants used either fresh or dry.
  • When substituting dry for fresh, use 1/3 the amount.

Hydrogenation: A process in which extra hydrogen atoms are pumped into unsaturated fat.

Ice Bath: A container of ice water used to stop the cooking process or cool foods or liquids quickly.

Jus: The natural juice of a meat, vegetable or fruit.

Jus Lie: Pan juices thickened with a slurry.

Julienne: Matchstick pieces of vegetables, fruits or cooked meats.

Kale: Curly-leafed vegetable from the cabbage family.

Kohlrabi: Root vegetable that resembles a turnip but has a more delicate flavor.

Larding: Threading strips of fat into a piece of meat before cooking.
  • Larding needle – hollow needle

Liaison: Thickening or binding agent used in the preparation of a soup or sauce.

Liaison Finale: Finishing or enriching agent added to soups or sauces at the end of the cooking process.

Madeira: Fortified wine, either sweet or dry, from the Portuguese island of Madeira.

Maillard Reaction: When natural sugars and proteins react to heat by caramelizing-browning and forming a crust.

Mandoline: A slicer with adjustable blades.

Marinade: A flavorful liquid used to tenderize and flavor products.
  • Usually includes an acid, oil, herbs and spices

Mince: To cut or chop into very fine particles.

Mirepoix: Rough cut flavorful vegetables– traditionally carrots, onions, celery and sometimes leeks.

Monder: To blanch, peel and seed tomatoes.

Monter au Beurre: To swirl small chunks of cold, whole butter into a sauce at the end of the cooking process.

Nage: A light sauce created from a court bouillon.

Nap: To lightly coat with a sauce or to cook a sauce until it coats the back of a spoon.

Organic Shapes: Shapes with a natural look and a flowing, curved appearance. Examples of organic shapes include the shapes of leaves, plants, and animals. In the food world this could be the natural shapes of strawberries, potato crisp, eggs, etc.

Pan-Fry: To cook in a moderate amount of fat; sauté.

Pan Gravy: Pan drippings thickened with flour.

Parboil: To boil until partially cooked; remainder of cooking is done by another method.

Pluches: Small sprigs of herbs

Poach: To gently simmer in liquid.

Purée: To sieve or whirl food into a smooth, thick mixture.

Quenelle: A neat, three-sided oval formed by smoothing a mixture between two spoons. A quenelle can be formed from foods such as chocolate mousse, whipped cream, polenta, mashed potato and so on.

Ragout: A rich stew.

Reduction: The result of boiling down liquids in order to concentrate flavors.

Remouillage: Second, weaker extraction made from the remnants of a stock.
- Half the water, half the cook time
- Used to start another stock

Render: To liquefy the fat from a meat product over low heat.
- Product should be diced or scored.

Resting: Letting a roast rest for 5 to 15 minutes after cooking.
- Equalizes internal pressure so juices can be re-absorbed
- Allows for carryover cooking

Roast: Oven-cook foods in an uncovered pan to produce a well-browned product with a moist interior.
- Dry cooking method
- Best for tender cuts of meat

Rondeau: Heavy pan with straight sides that are less than the width of the base. It is commonly used for braising.

Roux: A cooked combination of fat and flour used to thicken sauces and soups.

Sabayon: A mixture of egg yolks and an acid whisked over hot water just until the yolks start to thicken.

Sambal: A chile paste, often with garlic, salt, sugar and other spices, used in Asian cuisine.

Sauté: To cook quickly over high heat in a minimal amount of oil.

Sauternes: A fruity, sweet white wine from the Bordeaux region.

Scald: To heat milk just below the boiling point (tiny bubbles appear around the edge of the pan when it has reached the proper temperature).

Sear: To brown meat quickly either in a hot pan with very little oil or in a hot oven.

Shock: To stop the cooking process by plunging a food in ice water.

Simmer: To cook in liquid over low heat just below the boiling point (bubbles form slowly and burst before reaching the surface).

Singer: To dust with flour after sautéing or roasting – flour mixes with the fat to create a quick roux.

Skim: To remove fat or scum from the surface of a liquid with a spoon or ladel.

Slurry: 50/50 mixture of cold liquid and refined starch – most often arrowroot or cornstarch.

Smoke Point: The temperature at which oils begin to smoke, burn and/or break down.

Spices: Buds, fruits, flowers, bark, berries, seeds and roots of plants and trees, used as seasonings.

Star Anise: the brown, fragrant pod of a Chinese evergreen used as a spice.

Steam: To cook in water vapors, on a rack or in a steam basket, in a covered pan above boiling water.

Steep: To infuse in liquid.

Stew: To cook a product barely covered in a flavorful liquid until the product is tender.
  • Good for tough, small cuts of meat.
  • Usually completed on top of the stove.
  • Stewed vegetables are usually not seared.

Stir: Using a spoon or a whisk in a broad, circular motion, to mix ingredients without beating or to prevent them from sticking.

Sweat: To cook slowly over medium/low heat without browning.
  • Good for flavor extraction.
  • Moisture development encouraged.

Tamarind Concentrate: A sour-flavored paste made from the the pod of a tropical tree.

Texture: The structural quality of a food— roughness, smoothness, graininess, or creaminess.

Truss: Tie products prior to cooking.
  • Helps maintain a products shape.
  • Ensures even cooking.

Tuile: A thin, crisp, curved wafer.

Turmeric: The root of a musky-smelling tropical plant, used as a spice — usually used in powdered form.

Whip: To beat rapidly with a wire whisk, or electric mixer, incorporating air to lighten a mixture and increase its volume.

Whisk: To beat with a wire whisk until blended and smooth.

Whitewash: 50/50 mixture of cold liquid and flour.

Zest: Outer colored peel of citrus fruits. Also, the act of removing this outer peel.

Index